Orkneys

SCOTLAND

② ① ③ ④

STRATHCLYDE ⑤ ① (BERNICIA)

② ⑥ Hadrian's Wall ⑦

③ NORTHUMBRIA ④ (DIERA) ⑤ ⑦ ⑥

IRELAND ①

② ③ ④

① ② ③

NORTH WALES MERCIA ④

EAST ANGLIA

① ⑤ ① ②

⑩ ⑦ ⑥ ⑥ ② WESSEX ⑧ ⑨ ③ ③ ESSEX ①

⑤ ④ ① ④ ②

⑪ ② KENT

SUSSEX ① ③ ②

① ENGLISH CHANNEL

STRAITS OF DOVER

①

②

BRITTANY NORMANDY FRANCE (GAUL)

First published 1971
Macdonald & Co (Publishers) Limited
St Giles House, 49–50 Poland Street
London W1.
© Macdonald & Co
(Publishers) Limited, 1971
Made and printed by:
Hazell, Watson and Viney Ltd
Aylesbury
Bucks

Edited by Bridget Hadaway and
Sue Jacquemier

Cover designed by Robert Jackson

SBN 356 03750 9

Library of Congress
Catalog Card No.
78-169914

**We wish to thank the following
individuals and organisations for
their assistance and for making
available material in their
collections:**

Aerofilms Ltd *pages 7, 10, 19*

Allen, Julian *pages 2, 13*

American Heritage:
    Bibliothèque Nationale *page 63*
    Burgerbibliothek, Berne *page 61*
    Collection Kampmann,
      Copenhagen *page 68*
    Fairmount Park Art Association
      page 51
    Royal Library of Copenhagen
      page 53
    Statens Historiska Museum,
      Stockholm *page 66*

A.T.A. Stockholm *pages 49, 60, 66, 68*

Barnaby's Picture Library *pages 6, 16*

Batchelor, John *pages 26, 45*

Bodleian Library, Oxford *pages 1, 8, 28,
    29, 31, 42, 59, 65, 70, 71, 84*

Boyce, Peter *pages 17, 37*

Bristol City Museum *page 4*

Cambridge University Library *page 67*

Clayton, Peter *cover, pages 10, 15, 20, 34*

Colchester and Essex Museum *page 15*

Crown Copyright *pages 7, 17, 30, 32*

Davis, William Gordon *page 41*

The Dean and Chapter of Durham
    Cathedral Library *pages 42, 85*

The Dean and Chapter of Wells
    Cathedral: Christopher Ridley
    page 71

Devizes Museum *page 4*

Dixon, C. M. *pages 7, 25, 68*

Drury, Geoffrey *pages 11, 51*

Davidson, Ellis *page 49*

Hulton Picture Library *pages 1, 28, 33,
    37, 41, 54, 55, 56, 69, 70, 80*

Fassbind, Nicholas/Robertson, Alan
    page 74

Foto Marburg *pages 25, 26*

Lincoln Museum *page 4*

Lincoln's Inn Library *pages 73, 81*

Magnum: Erich Lessing *page 75*

Mansell Collection *pages 8, 9, 10, 11,
    14, 18, 19, 23, 24, 30, 40, 52, 67,
    82–3*

The Master and Fellows of Corpus
    Christi College, Cambridge *pages
    44, 64*

M.G.M. *page 59*

Michael Holford Library *cover, pages
    18, 33, 67, 68, 76, 77, 78*

Mittet Foto *cover, pages 1, 48*

Museo Civiltà Romana *page 10*

Museum of Antiquities of the
    University and the Society of
    Antiquaries of Newcastle-upon-
    Tyne *page 20*

National Museum of Ireland, Dublin
    page 63

National Museum of Wales *pages 4, 8*

National Portrait Gallery *page 61*

National Travel Association of
    Denmark: Jean Pierre Ducatez
    page 45

Newcastle Museum of Antiquities
    page 7

Oldsakamling University, Oslo
    pages 44, 50, 51

Pia, Jack *page 5*

Pictorial Colour Slides *page 17*

Pierpoint Morgan Library *page 62*

Public Record Office *page 84*

Ridley, Christopher *cover, pages 29, 72*

Royal Exchange: Geoffrey Drury
    page 54

Royal Library of Denmark *page 46*

Saye, L. J. A. *page 63*

Scala: Monte Cassino Abbey *page 81*

Science Museum, London *page 22*

St Albans Museum *page 19*

Snark International *page 43*

Stothard: Mark Gerson *page 85*

"Sunday Times" *page 19*

The Trustees of the British Museum
    *cover, pages 1, 4, 15, 17, 21, 31, 37,
    38, 39, 55, 57, 58, 61, 63, 70, 73, 85*

The Trustees of the London Museum
    pages 39, 51

Vana Haggerty *pages 5, 28*

Victoria and Albert Museum *page 72*

Wagstaff *page 38*

York Minster *page 34*

Macdonald
Educational

R J Unstead

Invaded Island

A Pictorial History
The Stone Age
to 1086

Volume One

The Invaded Island tells the story of the many invaders Britain has known. Its first inhabitants were Stone Age hunters who roamed the forests and hills in search of food; then came tribesmen who crossed the channel separating the island from the continent of Europe and settled on lands where they could farm, hunt and pasture their animals. In time, they or their descendants had to defend the lands they had occupied. This story was repeated over and over again. Invaders, armed as a rule with better weapons, would defeat the earlier settlers and occupy the more fertile parts of the island; then they would have to face attack by incoming tribes.

R J Unstead

Invaded Island

A Pictorial History
The Stone Age
to 1086

This warrior is an Ancient Briton, armed with a bronze-decorated shield and an iron-tipped spear, but he wears no armour. Warriors like this fought the Roman invaders when they first landed in Britain in 54 B.C.

Yet the Ancient Britons who lived in the south-east had crossed the English Channel from Gaul only a few years before the Romans came. In time, the Romans themselves had to defend the island they had conquered. Saxon pirates from across the sea raided the coasts of Britain. With their neighbours, the Angles and the Jutes, they settled the country and made it their own. Then came the terrible Norsemen, or Vikings, and after them, the Danes. The last of the successful invaders were the Norman knights led by William the Conqueror.

This book tells you about the invaders—how they fought and won the land, brought new ideas, and settled down in Britain, island of the West.

Contents

Britain's Early Peoples

Lions, elephants, rhinoceroses and sabre-toothed tigers once roamed the forests of Britain. A few wandering tribesmen lived on roots, berries and any small creatures they could catch. Gradually the climate became colder, and the land was covered with ice for thousands of years.

By about 9,000 B.C. the ice had melted again, and hunters from Denmark and France came searching for food. They were followed by farming people from further east who knew how to grow food and keep animals.

These early people used tools and weapons made of flint. Next came men who had learnt to make things out of a marvellous new substance called bronze, a mixture of copper and tin heated together. A few centuries later, people called the Celts came to Britain, bringing an even better, harder metal—iron.

This was the beginning of the Iron Age in Britain. The iron-using Celts were a proud, quarrelsome people. Different tribes were constantly fighting each other. When their neighbours over the sea, the Gauls, were attacked by the Romans, some of the Celts even went to help defend Gaul against the invaders.

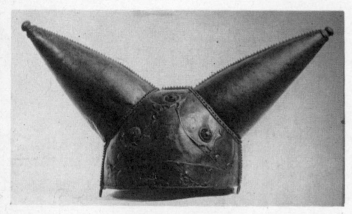
A warrior chief wore this helmet in about 100 B.C. His sword and spear-head were probably made of iron but helmets, shields, and many ornaments were still made of bronze. This helmet was found in the River Thames.

This razor-sharp arrowhead was made from flint in about 1500–1300 B.C. during the Bronze Age and was found in Wales.

This beaker which looks like a coffee mug was made by Bronze Age people called the Beaker folk, and was found in Denton, Lincs.

This bowl was once a solid piece of stone. Someone hollowed it out during the New Stone Age with a flint. It must have taken many months to do.

Girls and housewives used these carved weaving combs during the Early Iron Age. The combs are made of bone.

This little bronze boar was found near London. It was made about 2,000 years ago. Perhaps it was a lucky charm that would bring good luck in the boar-hunt, or perhaps it was made to remind the hunter of a particularly exciting kill.

4

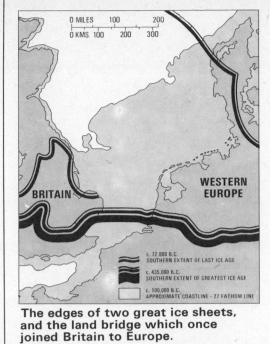

The edges of two great ice sheets, and the land bridge which once joined Britain to Europe.

Stone, Bronze and Iron Ages

Most of our knowledge of early man comes from the tools and weapons found in the ground. So the early periods of man's history are divided into "ages", named after the materials used at different times.

The Stone Age

The first tools and weapons were made of crude stone. Then man learnt to chip flint stones to make sharper edges.

For most of the Stone Age, the land now called Britain was joined to the continent of Europe. For long periods, great ice sheets covered the land. After the last great ice age the sea level rose, and Britain became an island cut off from Europe.

As the climate improved, great forests grew, in which men could hunt animals for food.

In the last period of the Stone Age, the Neolithic period, men began to farm and to make pots, houses and burial places.

The Bronze Age

This began in Britain about 2000 B.C. Men started to use copper, tin and then bronze. With these metals, they could make better weapons and tools.

The Iron Age

The use of iron seems to have reached Britain in about 750 B.C. although it was used much earlier in the Middle East. In Britain, Iron Age men made hill-forts, marsh villages and a primitive kind of money.

Homes of the early Britons

The earliest inhabitants of Britain lived in the open, in brushwood shelters, or in caves. They often made their homes near rivers and places where they could find flint for tools and weapons. They chipped these flints to make knives, hand-axes, and scrapers. They learnt to use fire to cook their meat and to frighten wild animals away.

Later on, men piled up stones to make houses like the ones in the pictures (below, left).

If there were no stones, men would make a circle with posts, and cover the posts with basketwork smeared with clay.

Some of the Britons built their homes on islands in lakes and marshes to make them safer from attack.

The picture below shows a house on Dartmoor. On the right hand side of the picture is a door with a curved windbreak, which gave protection from the weather.

The Pagan Island

Before they invaded the island, the Romans knew very little about Britain. It was supposed to lie on the fringes of the world, wrapped in mist, and inhabited by giants and demons.

This strange country was also said to be amazingly rich in gold, tin, and all kinds of metals, besides amber and corn.

Its people, of course, were barbarians. The Romans, who loved their own cruel sports, shuddered at tales of the islanders' savage customs. The Celts cut off their enemies' heads and nailed them up in their houses and temples; they drank out of skulls and made masks with huge eyes. They worshipped gods with horns and antlers, goddesses of battles and goddesses who ruled the woods and wild places.

Their priest-leaders, the Druids, were said to make human sacrifices and sprinkle altars with blood, and there were certain holy pools into which treasure was thrown to please the gods.

It was Julius Caesar, conqueror of Gaul, who finally decided that it was time that this rich mysterious land was brought under Roman rule.

Stonehenge

The greatest monument in western Europe stands on Salisbury Plain, eighty miles west of London.

Not much is known about the people who built Stonehenge, except that they started to build it in about 2000 B.C. They made a bank and a ditch to surround the temple and had raised some tall stones when for some reason the work stopped.

Presently, some new people arrived and made a fresh start; they actually managed to transport 80 huge stones right across country from south Wales, 180 miles away.

The temple consists of a circle of 30 tall stones with smaller stones laid across the tops. Inside the circle, was a group of trilithons (three stones, one lying across two uprights), a horseshoe arrangement of smaller stones and a huge stone usually known as the Altar Stone.

It seems likely that Stonehenge was the temple of a people who worshipped the sun. We know that they built and used it long before the Druids came to Britain.

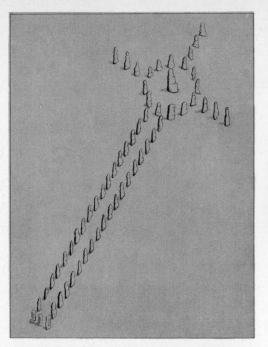

An ancient open-air temple in the shape of a cross, made of huge stones.

This ancient circle of stones, now overgrown, is in Ireland. It was probably used for ceremonies connected with the seasons of the year. Many Celtic remains have been found in Scotland and Ireland.

The Celts worshipped the human head. They even hung up the heads of their enemies in their temples. This stone head has a hollow in the top. It was used for pouring drinks for the gods of the Celts. Hundreds of Celtic skulls and heads made of stone and wood have been found.

Hill-forts

In this photograph you can see an old British hill-fort called Badbury Rings in Dorset. It is now overgrown with trees but at the end of the Stone Age it was a bare grassy hilltop. Neolithic men dug a circular ditch and threw the earth inwards to make a bank. They drove their cattle into the circle at night to protect them from wolves and robbers.

The later Bronze Age people were peaceful folk but, during the early part of the Iron Age, when warrior tribes arrived in Britain, the old hill-forts came back into use. Many new ones were made with three and four rings of ditches and strong banks called ramparts.

When enemies came up the hill to attack the fort, they were met by showers of stones and arrows. Piles of sling stones have been found as well as wrist-guards or "bracers" used by the bowmen. Hill-forts were found all over southern Britain.

Julius Caesar's Raids

Gaius Julius Caesar had conquered Gaul. In a bitter campaign, the general had defeated the warrior-tribesmen of France and Belgium. Now he was free to turn his attention to Britain.

The island interested him for a number of reasons. The Britons had been helping the Gauls and sheltering their defeated chiefs. With Gaul conquered, it might be necessary to conquer Britain as well. In any case, it would do no harm to impress the Britons with the power of Rome. The island was said to be fabulously rich and Caesar was anxious to send news of yet another dramatic triumph to Rome. He had powerful enemies in the city and wanted to keep his popularity with the common people. With all these things in mind, the general prepared an expeditionary force of two legions which would be carried across the Channel in eighty ships; a squadron of cavalry would follow.

At dawn, on an August morning in 55 B.C., the Roman fleet neared the cliffs of Dover. Caesar could see that this was no place for a landing and gave the order to sail along the coast, while the Britons raced along the cliff-tops, easily keeping pace

The Roman Empire

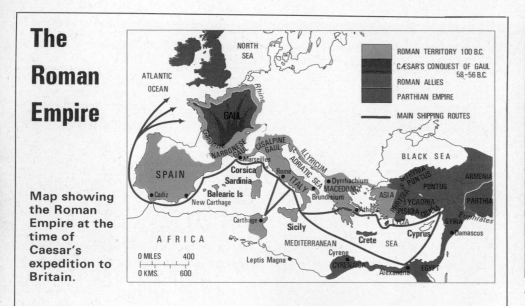

Map showing the Roman Empire at the time of Caesar's expedition to Britain.

The Roman Eagle, king of the birds and symbol of a great empire.

The Romans were a disciplined, warlike people from Italy. They conquered more and more land until they eventually built up an enormous empire.

By the time Caesar invaded Gaul, between 58 and 55 B.C. Spain and the other places coloured mauve on the map were already part of the empire.

The Roman people loved new victories and conquests.

The story of Caesar's victories in Gaul and Britain was written by Caesar himself. But since he wrote it to tell people what a marvellous general he was, he may have hidden the fact that his British expeditions were much less successful than he had hoped.

Julius Caesar, one of the greatest generals in history, was 47 when he first invaded Britain in 55 BC. He was murdered in 44 B.C.

The Britons who fought Caesar were experts in chariot fighting. They raced into battle in chariots like the one above. Some warriors balanced on the poles in front. They leapt down to fight on foot.

with the slow-moving vessels. By afternoon, the Romans found themselves opposite an open beach and when they ran their ships ashore, the Britons were already at the water's edge. After a bloody struggle the legionaries fought their way ashore and advanced in a solid disciplined mass, armoured, helmeted, protected by their shields. The Britons broke and fled. Caesar, whose cavalry had not arrived, ordered the troops to make camp.

Next day, the Britons came asking for peace and offering gifts but while talks were going on, a storm damaged some of the Roman ships and the Britons withdrew and made a fierce attack upon the enemy camp. Caesar managed to beat them off and embark his troops to safety in Gaul.

It was a humiliating failure but, next year, Caesar came back with a bigger army, pressed inland, crossed the Thames and captured the Britons' stronghold at Wheathampstead. When their chiefs asked for peace, he readily agreed, because he had heard news of a revolt in Gaul and dared not stay any longer. He never came back, and the Britons saw no more Roman soldiers for nearly a hundred years.

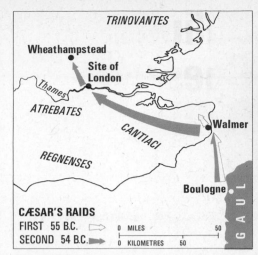

The map above shows Caesar's two short invasions of Britain. The mauve arrows show how much further his troops advanced on their second expedition than on the first. Gaul, where they started from, lies just across the sea from Britain.

The heroic standard-bearer

As Caesar's ships approached the shore of Britain, his men could see that they were faced by hordes of excited warriors, brandishing spears and making ready to dash into the surf. The Roman legionaries hesitated. They had had no experience of fighting against war chariots drawn up on the beach. At this moment, the Standard-bearer of the tenth legion cried out, "Jump, lads, unless you wish to lose your Eagle. Follow me!" He plunged into the waves and the soldiers, appalled by the prospect of losing their sacred emblem, leapt after him.

Claudius Conquers Britain

Eighty-seven years after Julius Caesar withdrew his troops, a much more powerfully equipped army set out for Britain. Its conquest had been ordered by the Emperor Claudius, who appointed Aulus Plautius as his general.

The army advanced quickly from the Kent coast to the River Medway, where they found the Britons waiting on the other side. A detachment of soldiers swam across the river, catching the Britons by surprise. After fierce fighting, the Britons were defeated, and the Romans, now joined by Claudius himself, marched on into Essex.

There they captured Camulodunum (Colchester), stronghold of the British leader Caractacus. Many chiefs surrendered, but further inland the invaders met stiff opposition. It took them four years to subdue all the tribes of the Midlands and the South. Supported by the fighting tribes of Yorkshire and Wales, Caractacus carried on the struggle until he was finally defeated and sent as a prisoner to Rome. Paraded through the streets, he is said to have shown such defiant courage that the Emperor spared his life.

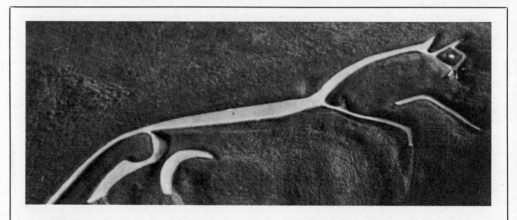

'Cymbeline'

After they had conquered Gaul, just across the sea from Britain, the Romans always tried to keep at least one big tribe in the south of Britain friendly to them, to prevent the Britons uniting against them.

Cunobelinus, king (or chief) of one of the largest tribes, upset the Romans' plans by conquering neighbouring tribes and building up his own little empire.

The great white horse in the picture above was cut into a hillside in Britain. It was the symbol of Cunobelinus's tribe.

Cunobelinus (called "Cymbeline" by Shakespeare) died at about the time when Claudius became Emperor in Rome. His sons carried on expanding his "empire" until they were defeated by Claudius's invading army.

Much of our knowledge of Britain between the invasions of Caesar and Claudius comes from coins. Different tribes and kings made different coins. The one above has the face of "Cymbeline" on it.

Some of the best troops in the Roman army were in the Praetorian Guards. This is their own special standard and is decorated with the honours they won. Claudius was a firm favourite with these guards.

The Romans found elephants very useful in war, especially for carrying baggage. Claudius took a number of these animals with him when he invaded Britain. The tribesmen, who had never seen such gigantic animals, were terrified by the sight of them.

Above is a model of Roman London as it developed after the Roman conquest of the southern part of Britain. The Romans always turned the places they conquered into Roman provinces, with Roman-style towns, roads, bridges and forts. The Romans were very good builders.

The Emperor who Stuttered

The Emperor Claudius, the stuttering child who grew up to become Emperor—and to command the expedition which conquered Britain.

When Claudius was a young boy his family never dreamt he would ever be fit to be an emperor. He limped, he was often ill, he rolled his head from side to side, and he had a bad stutter.

But he had a brilliant brain and he even wrote history while he was still a teenager.

Much later, the reigning Roman Emperor, Caligula, who was Claudius's own nephew, was murdered. To everyone's surprise, the soldiers of the Praetorian Guard decided to make Claudius Emperor of Rome.

Since it was the soldiers who had made him Emperor, Claudius decided to win their respect by proving that he could be a great military commander. This was why he ordered the invasion of Britain.

It was now almost a hundred years since Caesar's brief expeditions to Britain. The island was still unconquered, but the Romans now knew much more about it, and in the south-east, some of the British chiefs had begun to adopt Roman ways. Claudius also had very good generals. So this time the Romans were able to conquer Britain in fairly easy, well planned stages.

Claudius reigned successfully for thirteen years. He died in A.D. 54, poisoned by mushrooms given to him by his fourth wife, who murdered him so that her son Nero could become Emperor in his place.

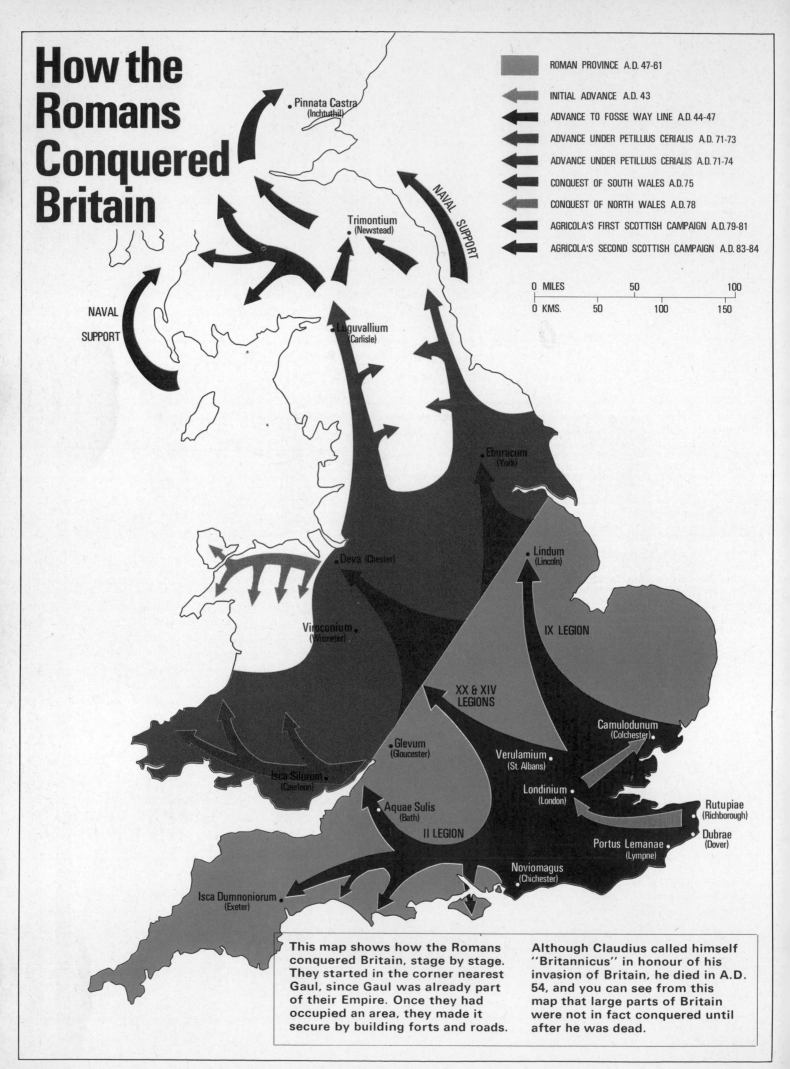

How the Romans Conquered Britain

Legend:
- ROMAN PROVINCE A.D. 47-61
- INITIAL ADVANCE A.D. 43
- ADVANCE TO FOSSE WAY LINE A.D. 44-47
- ADVANCE UNDER PETILLIUS CERIALIS A.D. 71-73
- ADVANCE UNDER PETILLIUS CERIALIS A.D. 71-74
- CONQUEST OF SOUTH WALES A.D. 75
- CONQUEST OF NORTH WALES A.D. 78
- AGRICOLA'S FIRST SCOTTISH CAMPAIGN A.D. 79-81
- AGRICOLA'S SECOND SCOTTISH CAMPAIGN A.D. 83-84

0 MILES 50 100
0 KMS. 50 100 150

Pinnata Castra (Inchtuthil)

NAVAL SUPPORT

Trimontium (Newstead)

NAVAL SUPPORT

Luguvallium (Carlisle)

Eburacum (York)

Deva (Chester)

Lindum (Lincoln)

IX LEGION

Viroconium (Wroxeter)

XX & XIV LEGIONS

Camulodunum (Colchester)

Glevum (Gloucester)

Verulamium (St. Albans)

Isca Silurum (Caerleon)

Londinium (London)

Rutupiae (Richborough)

Aquae Sulis (Bath)

II LEGION

Dubrae (Dover)

Portus Lemanae (Lympne)

Noviomagus (Chichester)

Isca Dumnoniorum (Exeter)

This map shows how the Romans conquered Britain, stage by stage. They started in the corner nearest Gaul, since Gaul was already part of their Empire. Once they had occupied an area, they made it secure by building forts and roads.

Although Claudius called himself "Britannicus" in honour of his invasion of Britain, he died in A.D. 54, and you can see from this map that large parts of Britain were not in fact conquered until after he was dead.

The Roman Soldier

1 Helmet, made of either bronze or iron with leather cheek pieces. The Latin for helmet is *cassis*. A legionary would wear a badge on his *cassis* for ceremonial parades.

2 Armour, made of metal strips fastened together. The strips are curved around the shoulders and across the chest. They are laced in front and hinged at the back.

3 Tunic and scarf are worn to save skin from getting sore.

4 Heavy javelin, or *pilum*, 7 ft long, with pointed end to stick in ground. Each soldier carried two javelins.

5 Dagger, or *pugio*. This one measures from nine inches to ten inches.

6 Belts, tunics, boots, aprons and breeches are made of leather. Thongs of the apron have metal plates all the way down, and bronze weights on the end of each thong. Apron hangs from the belt.

7 Two-edged sword, or *gladius* : 2 ft long.

8 Shield made of sheets of wood with iron or bronze at the edges : held by a handgrip on the inside.

9 Boots, or heavy leather sandals, with metal studs on the soles.

Britain's First Heroine

Boadicea's husband, King of the Iceni, had been friendly with the Romans. But when he died, they tried to take over his kingdom. Boadicea and her daughters protested at this but the Roman commander refused to listen. This insult aroused the old fighting spirit of the Iceni. Seizing swords and spears, they killed the hated officials and, with Boadicea at their head, they attacked Colchester and looted the town. Boadicea's army was joined by hordes of other tribesmen, all swearing to wipe out every trace of Roman rule. They smashed the Ninth Legion, burnt London to the ground and sacked the fine new city of St Albans, slaughtering every man, woman and child in the place.

When the Roman Governor heard of the revolt he ordered the legions to march and subdue the rebels. Urged on by their Queen, the Britons dashed at the Roman line, hurling themselves again and again at the enemy's tight-locked front. The Roman veterans stood fast. Better armed, they drove the Britons back and slaughtered them. The revolt was over and Britain was a secure province of Rome again.

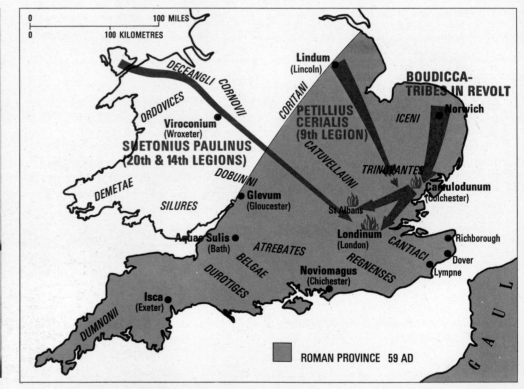

Boadicea was the wife of King Prasutagus of the Iceni tribe. After the defeat of her rebellion against the Romans, she and her daughters escaped to the woods. There, in despair, they drank poison. Neither her tomb nor that of her daughters has ever been found.

She was Britain's first heroine and in her veins ran the fierce, warlike, independent blood of the Britons. Her bravery has seldom been equalled.

This map shows where Boadicea (also known as Boudicca) fought her battles against the Romans.

The parts coloured mauve show the parts of Britain the Romans ruled in A.D. 59. The white parts were not yet under Roman rule.

The dark green arrows show the places Boadicea's army came from and some of the places where she fought.

The blue arrows show how the Roman legions marched at top speed from miles outside Roman territory under their commanders, Suetonius Paulinus and Petilius Cerialis.

The red flames show where the biggest battles were fought. The artist has drawn flames because many houses and buildings were burnt to the ground.

Both sides behaved with hideous cruelty. Boadicea's forces are said to have killed 70,000 people in and around St Albans alone, and the Romans massacred their defeated enemies without mercy.

The huge numbers of Britons who fought and died in Boadicea's rebellion show how much they hated their Roman conquerors.

A child at Colchester must have played with these toys in the first century B.C. They were found in his grave which was dug around the time of Boadicea's brave revolt.

The Roman army

The Roman army was successful because it made sure that it was better trained, better armed and better disciplined than any of its adversaries.

The army was made up of legions. A legion contained between 3,000 and 6,000 men. The ordinary soldiers were called legionaries (the soldier on page 13 is a legionary). The legionary was the backbone of the Roman army. As the Empire grew, more and more of the "Roman" soldiers were recruited from the conquered countries. Britons, for example, served in the Roman army—but always far away from their homes.

Each legion was divided into ten cohorts. A cohort was, in turn, divided into centuries. Each century was a company of a hundred. The leaders of the centuries were called centurions. The words "century" and "centurion" come from the Latin word *centum* (written C), meaning one hundred. Each legion had an eagle standard which it carried into battle. Each cohort had its own badge, called a *signum*.

The emperor himself had his own bodyguard. This was called the Praetorian Guard, and at times was so powerful that it even elected the emperor. Claudius was elected emperor by the Praetorian Guard.

There were also auxiliaries, who were archers, dart-throwers, camel-corps and cavalry.

Nero

Nero was the Roman Emperor at the time of Boadicea's rebellion. The gold coin above has his head stamped on it.

Nero became emperor at the age of 17. For a time he behaved well because he had a wise teacher named Seneca. When he had been reigning for ten years, a fire destroyed most of Rome. Nero gave help to the poor who had lost their homes and rebuilt the city in magnificent style. But when rumours went round that Nero himself had started the fire, he put the blame on the Christians, and persecuted them with terrible cruelty. He became so wicked that the army refused to protect him, and when the Senate ordered him to be executed, he committed suicide.

As well as the eagle standard, each legion had its own emblem. This boar, which is ready to charge, was the emblem of the Twentieth Legion. Under its commander Paulinus, this legion defeated Boadicea's brave troops.

LEG XX means Legion 20. The letter X is ten in Roman numerals. Other Roman numerals are:

I stands for 1
II stands for 2
III stands for 3
IV stands for 4
V stands for 5
IX stands for 9
L stands for 50
C stands for 100
D stands for 500
M stands for 1,000

Hadrian's Wall

Imagine a wall 73 miles long and 21 feet high, wide enough on top for 2 men to walk side by side, 16 great forts set in the wall about 5 miles apart, smaller "castles" every mile and 2 watch-towers between each pair of these mile-castles! These are just a few of the statistics of Hadrian's Wall which ran right across the northern neck of England.

The Emperor Hadrian who came to Britain in A.D. 122 built the wall "to separate the Romans from the barbarians". The Romans had failed to conquer the fierce Picts and Scots who lived in Caledonia (Scotland). The country seemed to have no riches of its own and the tribesmen's favourite occupation was raiding the southern farmlands. So the order was given to keep them out. This was Hadrian's policy. He made up his mind that the empire was big enough; inside its borders, he wanted law and order, trade, towns and splendid buildings. The barbarians, who understood none of these things, must be kept out. The wall baffled the Picts and Scots for seventy years. It was a barrier against Rome's enemies, and a new frontier of the Empire.

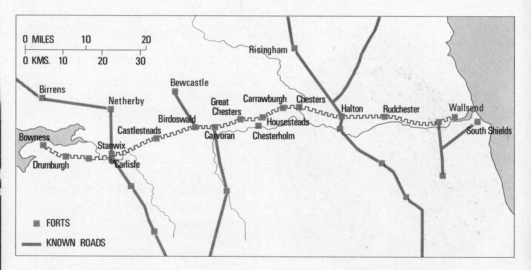

Rome's north-west frontier

The Romans always preferred to have frontiers to their Empire which were easy to defend. Most of the other frontiers were either on the sea, on rivers, or in deserts, which attackers would find difficult to cross. Since there was no natural barrier in the north of England, they had to build an artificial one, Hadrian's great Wall.

Hadrian's Wall is one of the most striking Roman remains in Britain. Much of it can still be seen stretching across northern England, near the Scottish border. The picture on the left shows a part of the Wall as it looks today.

The map shows the position of the Wall. The little mauve squares are forts, where the Roman soldiers stayed and from where they could dash out to fight off any northern

"barbarians" trying to cross to the south.

The grey lines are roads along which the Romans could bring up reinforcements. They also built some roads and forts to the north of the Wall. This made it harder for the "barbarians" to reach the Wall, let alone climb over it.

The emperor after Hadrian, called Antoninus Pius, decided to build a second wall further to the north. This wall was made of turf, and was therefore much less strong than Hadrian's Wall, so it had to be abandoned after about forty years.

Although Hadrian's Wall was an immensely strong defence, it was crossed many times by the northern "barbarians". This usually happened when some of the Roman soldiers had been withdrawn to fight in another part of the Empire.

The Romans carved many statues of their gods and of animals in bronze, marble and limestone. This splendid lion (left) was found on Hadrian's Wall.

The soldiers guarding the Wall stored many of their provisions in granaries. The picture above shows the ruins of a granary.

This bronze mask had a thin covering of gold. It would have been worn by Romans on ceremonial occasions. It was found on Hadrian's Wall.

All kinds of fascinating ruins, carvings and other objects have been found on and near Hadrian's Wall. Many Roman soldiers lived in and near the forts on the Wall for long periods of time. The things they left behind have been carefully studied by archaeologists and historians.

The picture (top right) shows the system of drains, lavatories and washing arrangements organised by the soldiers who guarded the Wall. The picture above shows a temple which the Romans dedicated to the sun god, Mithras.

Life in Roman Britain

The Romans never conquered the whole of Britain. They built Hadrian's Wall and manned the army bases at York, Chester and Caerleon (in South Wales) to control the unruly tribes of the north and west. But they did not try to pacify those outlying areas. In the south and the Midlands, however, life was peaceful and orderly. Here were neat, well laid-out towns, country villas, fields of grain, and the bustle of a Roman province.

The architects and town-planners who arrived with the army knew exactly what was wanted, because they had planned countless towns all over the Empire. First, they chose a site near to the old tribal centre of the district and marked out a rectangular area which was divided up by streets neatly crossing at right-angles. Spaces were chosen for the *Forum* or market-place, the temples, law-courts, council chambers and barracks. Other spaces were filled in with shops, private houses, public baths and sometimes an amphitheatre for plays, shows and sporting events. The town was protected by a wall and massive gateways.

When the first towns of this kind went up, the Roman Governor had to encourage Britons to go and live in them.

This is a face of a god or spirit of autumn—his head crowned with leaves and fruits. He is part of a magnificent mosaic floor discovered at Cirencester (Gloucestershire). "Mosaic" is a way of setting small cubes of coloured stone in cement to make a pattern or a picture. The Romans employed expert workers, usually slaves, to make the beautiful mosaic floors which have been found in many places and which give us an idea of the luxurious homes of wealthy citizens in Britain. Every home had its household gods—the god of the doorway, the goddess of the hearth, the god of abundance and so on—who brought good luck and happiness to the family.

Shopping in Roman Britain
Here you can see two shop-assistants holding up a piece of cloth for a customer's inspection. Shops were quite small, more like stalls than our modern shops. A house owner would often let a street-level room of his house as a shop; goods inside might be pottery, wine, olive-oil, cutlery or cloth.

Roman Britain produced lead, copper, tin, iron and some silver and gold, but the island was not as rich as the Romans imagined. The Britons were fine workers in bronze and coloured enamels. Wheat was widely grown; British oysters, pearls, hunting-dogs, woollen cloaks and blankets were well-known, but, although there were several pottery factories in Britain, the best earthenware and glass were imported.

Leading men of the district were told to move there with their families and work people. Their sons were taught to read and write Latin, to speak in the lawcourt and council chamber; other boys learnt how to measure and calculate, how to make cement and build with stone and brick, how to run a business and, of course, how to pay taxes and obey the laws. In less than twenty years, the Romans changed the British warriors into town-dwellers. Most of the peasants went on working on the land as if nothing had happened; they spoke the Celtic language and probably understood only a few Latin words they picked up when they took produce to market.

A network of roads covered the country. These roads were built so that troops could march swiftly to any trouble-spot; they also allowed messengers and officials to travel about the Empire and merchants to transport their goods. But the Romans did not let their roads become choked by heavy wagons; the Car Dyke, for example, was dug from Cambridge to Lincoln and into the river Trent, so that corn could be taken by inland waterways as far north as York.

Fashionable ladies wore their hair in curls and coiled plaits which were held in position by heavy combs like these. They also used eyebrow-tweezers and manicure sets.

This is a model of the palace-villa at Fishbourne in Sussex. It was built for Cogidumnus, chief of a local tribe, who quickly made friends with the Roman conquerors and even changed his own name to Tiberius Claudius! Only a very rich man could have afforded a house of this size and splendour. The pillared entrance leads into a courtyard surrounded by elegant buildings which contain halls, bedrooms, bathrooms, kitchens, stores and slaves' quarters. The covered walk running along the fronts of the buildings served as a corridor.

The open-air theatre at Verulamium (St Albans) was used for plays, dancing, wrestling, bear-baiting and cock-fights. Magistrates and priests sat in the front row with the spectators seated behind them on banked rows of stone seats.

Farmhouse-villa at Lullingstone, Kent, in about A.D. 360. Looking rather like a big bungalow, it contained living-rooms with glazed windows, bathroom and Christian chapel; the kitchen and granary were separate buildings. The owners were wealthy farmers.

A Great Many Gods

The Romans were usually very broadminded about religion. They worshipped a great many gods, goddesses, spirits and nymphs of their own and, when they conquered a country, they rarely interfered with its religion. Often, they adopted a local god, such as Isis of Egypt and Mithras, who came originally from Persia. After the death of Julius Caesar, the emperors themselves were often raised to the level of gods.

On public holidays people were expected to honour the official Roman gods—Jupiter, Minerva, the emperors and so on—and if they did so, no-one minded much about other gods. Hence, the Britons were able to go on worshipping their own Celtic gods—Brigantia, Andate, Sul, Coventina the water nymph, and many others. Christianity reached Britain some time in the second century and must have spread quickly, because by A.D. 310 there were churches, chapels, priests and bishops. From time to time, an Emperor would have the Christians persecuted, but, for long periods, Christians and pagans lived side by side without quarrelling.

Tiberius, god-emperor, who succeeded Augustus.

Emperor-worship

Emperor-worship was introduced by Caesar Augustus who felt that if people made offerings before an image of the emperor, they would feel loyal to Rome, no matter what their race or what other gods they worshipped. So this became the official religion and every town had to have a temple to the emperors, living and dead, which were spoken of as "the Divine House". Games and festivals were held in their honour and had to be paid for by a group of rich citizens. A new building and even a temple to another god would be dedicated to the emperor. Worship of Claudius was specially popular in Britain and his temple at Colchester, which was destroyed by Boadicea's rebels, was rebuilt in magnificent style.

Roman gods

Romans believed they were surrounded by spirits who guarded the home if they had gifts of food and wine. Besides these household gods, there was also *Jupiter*, god of rain, thunder and lightning. He was Lord of the Heavens, Giver of Victory and Protector of Rome.

In their conquests, the Romans came across many new gods and, instead of offending them, they often added them to their own religion. Thus, the Greeks provided them with a whole family of gods and goddesses; here are the chief ones with their Roman names:

Jupiter King of the gods
Juno wife of Jupiter
Mars god of war
Minerva goddess of wisdom
Neptune the sea-god
Diana the huntress
Vulcan god of fire
Vesta goddess of the hearth
Saturn, *Ceres* god and goddess of crops
Janus two-faced god of the doorway
Venus goddess of love.

After Julius Caesar's time, the emperors were declared gods and, since it was wrong to disobey a god, soldiers usually remained loyal to the emperor.

Some foreign gods which be-

This carved silver plaque shows Sylvanus hanging rabbits on a tree. Sylvanus, one of the oldest and best-loved gods, was a woodland spirit, protector of shepherds, huntsmen and cattle. He was also known as Faunus, and, in Greece, as Pan. He was said to have horns and the legs of a goat, but here he takes the shape of a man and is accompanied by his little hunting-dog.

came popular in the Empire were *Isis* and *Osiris* (Egypt), *Astoreth* (Phoenicia), *Mithras* (Persia) and *Jesus Christ* (Judaea).

Christianity in Britain

This fourth century mosaic found at Hinton St Mary, Dorset, almost certainly shows the head of Christ between two pomegranates. We can be certain that the picture was made for a Christian household because of the sign like an X with the letter P: this is a *Chi-Rho* monogram; in other words, the first two letters of Christ's name in Greek. The monogram was often used by Christians as a secret sign, scratched perhaps on a wall, added to a picture or to an old tomb used as an altar. In times of persecution, the Christians would go into hiding and would hold services in private chapels and underground places. It was during one of those periods, perhaps in the reign of Diocletian, that Saint Alban, Britain's first martyr, was executed. Alban, a rich citizen of Verulamium (St Albans), gave shelter to a Christian priest for long enough to be converted to the new religion, and later he dressed himself in the priest's robe in order to allow the refugee to escape from his pursuers. The Roman governor ordered Alban to be beheaded, not so much because he was a Christian, but because he refused to honour the Roman gods and therefore the emperor himself. At the place of Alban's execution, a spring appeared from the spot where he died on a hill known to this day as Holywell.

Most Romans did not find it difficult to believe that a man (such as an emperor) could become a god, nor that the Christians' god should come to earth as a man; what was hard to understand was the obstinate belief by the Christians that there was no other god except Jesus Christ who had been executed in the province of Judaea during the reign of Tiberius.

The Threat to the Empire

While the legions patrolled the Wall and manned the border forts, Britain was safe. But, if, for some reason, troops were sent away to another part of the Empire, then the barbarians swept down from the hills to plunder the towns and the country villas. This happened several times between about A.D. 230 and 280, when Saxon pirates also began to raid the east coast for slaves, cattle and jewelled loot. But Rome struck back. Fresh troops, new defences and better rulers saved the province and all was well for another fifty years. By 350, however, the Picts were raiding the northern border, the Scots (still based in Ireland) were attacking the western coasts and more Saxons came plundering the east. In 367, the defences snapped and the army was heavily defeated but, although the Empire was under attack all along its frontiers, the Romans would not abandon Britain. They went on sending soldiers and ships to protect the province until they could send no more and, in 410, the Emperor Honorius had to tell the Britons they must fight for themselves because he needed every soldier to defend Italy and the city of Rome itself from the barbarian hordes.

One of the squadrons of Roman warships which guarded the Saxon Shore.

The Saxon Shore forts; similar ones were built further north and in the west.

The sea defences

When Claudius invaded Britain, the Romans built a small fort at Richborough (Sandwich), their main port of entry. That fort is still there, with the remains of a monument put up in honour of the conquest. For many years the port needed no other defences until, in the third century, the original fort was surrounded by much higher, thicker walls. This stronger fort was part of a new chain of defences, and you can see on this map the names of similar forts built along the east and south coast of Britain— the Saxon Shore, as it was called. Set on cliff-tops and beside river mouths, these forts were bases and look-out posts for soldiers and for the British fleet—the *Classis Britannica*—which, in twelve or more squadrons, patrolled the waters of the Saxon Shore in order to repel the constant attacks of barbarian pirates. The commander of these land and sea defences was known as the Count of the Saxon Shore. In the fourth century similar forts were built as far north as Yorkshire.

Above is a sculptor's picture of a squadron of Roman war-galleys; can you work out the number of oars to each galley and the probable number of rowers? Notice the high, curved prows and sterns, and the pointed beaks for ramming the enemy. What do you think the little "castles" were for and how were the galleys steered? One of the Roman admirals, Carausius, was accused of waiting to intercept the raiders on their way home, so that he could share the booty with them! He set himself up as "Emperor" of Britain, and retained power for six years until he was murdered.

Ivory carving of Stilicho, perhaps the last great general of the Western Empire.

The last great general

Stilicho was a German and a Christian, and one of the last Roman generals. In about 392, he became guardian to the young Honorius, made him emperor and ruled for him. A barbarian people called the Goths had broken into the Empire but Stilicho defeated them in Greece and Northern Italy, sent troops to strengthen the province of Britain and is said to have come himself to carry out a naval raid on the Picts and the Irish. In 402, however, the danger to Italy was so great that he had to withdraw troops from Britain. He won a great victory over the Germanic tribes, but his successes alarmed the Emperor and Stilicho was murdered in 408; and soon afterwards the Goths captured Rome.

Hengist promises to beat the Picts and to give his daughter in marriage to Vortigern

Vortigern's false ally

Vortigern is supposed to have been a prince of south-east Britain in about the year 450, some 40 years after the Roman troops had gone. By now, the Picts were raiding far into the southern part of the island and Vortigern is said to have offered pay to a Germanic tribe called the Jutes if they would drive the Picts back. When the Jutes had done so, their leaders, Hengist and Horsa, refused to go home. Instead, they chased the Britons out of Kent and settled down there with their followers.

23

The Capture of Rome

Why did the Roman Empire collapse? Why was that marvellous organisation wrecked by hordes of savages who knew almost nothing about building, law, art, poetry and trade?

There were many reasons: the Empire decayed in its heart—in Italy and in Rome itself. The government was weak; the Emperor was often feeble, wicked or mad and no-one knew who would succeed him. So while the generals fought each other for power, judges, senators and officials became greedy and dishonest. The population was falling and there were simply not enough Romans to run an empire. The people scorned work and left it to the slaves, for they preferred sport and luxuries; when the conquests stopped, less wealth flowed to Rome, though everyone groaned about the taxes.

Meanwhile, beyond the borders of the Empire, the barbarians were on the move. They pressed in from the steppes of Asia, eventually, they broke through the lines of the frontier and overran the Empire. But this did not happen suddenly. Rome was 400 years growing and another 400 years dying.

The barbarians capture Rome The year is A.D. 410, the barbarians are the Visigoths and this is a nineteenth-century artist's idea of how their king, Alaric, led them into the city, which they pillaged for six days. As a matter of fact, they probably looked much less savage than this, because they had long been in touch with Roman ways and Alaric, himself a Christian, had served the Emperor Theodosius for a time. Twice defeated and driven out of Italy by Stilicho, Alaric returned as soon as he heard of the general's murder. His army burst into the city where Alaric allowed his men to load themselves with treasures, but he would not let them burn the buildings or massacre the inhabitants. Shortly afterwards, when he was only thirty-four, Alaric died in southern Italy and his men killed the servants who buried him, so the Romans would never find his body.

Here, from the side of an ancient tomb, is a Pictish huntsman with his dog; or perhaps he is driving off the herds of the Britons.

The Britons' appeal to Rome

The departure of the legions left the Britons virtually defenceless against the warlike tribes living north of the wall. An old historian named Gildas, described how the "foul hosts" of the Picts and Scots, with their "lust for blood" and their "hang-dog faces" covered with hair, pulled the Britons down from the Wall and slaughtered them "as lambs by butchers". He described how the Britons sent a letter to Rome begging for help in these words: "The barbarians drive us to the sea; the sea drives us to the barbarians; between these two methods of death, we are either massacred or drowned." But they got no help.

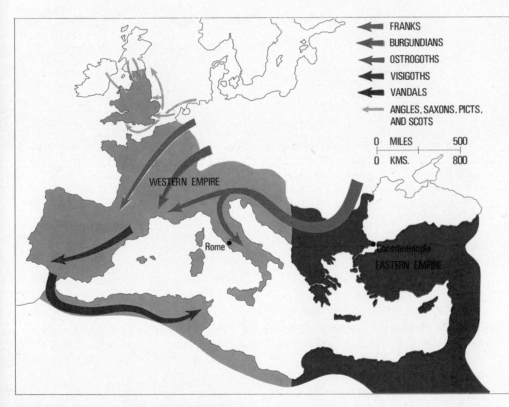

FRANKS
BURGUNDIANS
OSTROGOTHS
VISIGOTHS
VANDALS
ANGLES, SAXONS, PICTS, AND SCOTS

| 0 | MILES | 500 |
| 0 | KMS. | 800 |

WESTERN EMPIRE
Rome
Constantinople
EASTERN EMPIRE

What a contrast between this crude carving and the magnificent statues and mosaics of Roman art! It was probably made in about A.D. 500 and shows a Saxon chieftain with his spear. The dead were cremated and their ashes placed in burial urns; later, they were buried, men with their spears and combs, women with brooches, bronze toothpicks and ear-scoops.

Britain is cut off from Rome

This map shows clearly how impossible it was for the Romans to help Britain in the fifth century when the Empire was under desperate pressure, since the northern frontiers had been breached. The whole of the Western Empire was overrun by barbarians—first, the Vandals and the Visigoths (Western Goths), then the Franks and the Burgundians pressed in after them, driving them into Spain and North Africa, while the Ostrogoths (or Eastern Goths) poured into Greece and Italy from the Black Sea area.

In order to reach Britain, the legions would have been faced with the impossible task of fighting their way right across Gaul. By this time, as you can see, the island was being attacked from all sides, by tribesmen from Ireland, by the savage Picts who had overrun Hadrian's Wall and by Saxon raiders who ravaged the southern and eastern coasts.

The End of Roman Britain

Roman Britain suffered crisis after crisis before its rulers finally departed. As early as 196 the Governor Albinus took the army to Gaul in a bid to make himself emperor and Septimus Severus had to come back to crush the northern tribes who had burst through the defences. Emperor Severus rebuilt Hadrian's Wall and, when he died at York in 211, he had established peace that lasted for seventy years. Britain was now divided into two provinces to prevent any governor becoming too strong but, presently, Saxon pirates became so active in the North Sea that an officer named Carausius was appointed admiral to deal with them. Having driven them off and enriched himself with captured booty, he set up as emperor and ruled the island for six years until, in 293, he was murdered by a rival. As usual, the northern tribes took advantage of the situation, but a general named Chlorus arrived from Gaul to restore order. He sailed up the Thames and was welcomed as a deliverer by the London citizens. After the defences had been overhauled, a period of prosperity followed, with good government, revived trade and even a building boom, for many new houses, shops and villas

This Germanic carving shows Odin, lord of the Teutonic gods, wearing a helmet and armed with shield, sword and spear. Also known as Woden and Wotan, he was the god of war, "the raging one", and was attended by wolves and two ravens. His wife was Frigga and their son, Balder, was god of light.

Who were the Angles and Saxons?

Basically, they were one race of warrior-farmers from the low-lying plains and marshlands of Germany (Lower Saxony), Jutland and southern Denmark. They were tall and strong, fair-haired and blue-eyed—great fighting-men who loved fighting, jewellery and meat-eating beyond all else and, after these, farming. The Angles reached Britain by working along the German coast, crossing the Straits of Dover and pushing up the east coast to settle in Norfolk and Suffolk (the East Angles) and in the midland counties round Huntingdonshire (Middle Angles). The fierce Saxons followed the same route in order to settle in Essex (East Saxons), Middlesex (Middle Saxons) and Sussex (South Saxons); others pressed farther along the coast to found the kingdom of the West Saxons (Wessex). In the early days of the invasion, they were all more or less allies; after all, they were kinsmen and fellow-adventurers and there was no point in quarrelling when there was land enough for everyone who could carry sword and spear against the unwarlike Britons. This was no organised invasion, merely a steady inflow of settlers. Armed bands came ashore to win a foothold by cunning and strength. Doubtless, the local princes rallied their people and fought back, but the pressure was on, pressure that forced them always a little further west.

were constructed. But disaster was never far away and, in 376, the Saxons, Picts and Scots made a concerted onslaught. They defeated the army, ransacked the villas and overran the countryside, yet, once again, Rome came to the rescue. Theodosius was despatched to the troublesome island with a fresh army to repair the Wall and build signal forts to keep a watch against sea-raiders. The peace was short-lived, for Magnus Maximus was the next commander to take the troops away to Gaul and, in their absence, the Wall was finally overrun. The end was near. Though the valiant Stilicho checked the raiders, he had to recall many troops in his attempts to protect Rome itself. In 405 the army mutinied and, five years later, the Britons were told to fend for themselves. That they did not immediately collapse is shown by the visit in 429 of St Germanus, a French bishop, who found the islanders prosperous and still defending themselves. However, by mid-century, the Jutes had seized Kent and the Angles and Saxons were beginning to settle on farmlands they had wrested from the defeated Britons.

The longboat (from an example found at Nydam in Denmark), the kind of ship in which the Anglo-Saxon invaders made crossings to Britain. Narrow-beamed, low-sided, clinker-built, i.e. made of overlapping planks, probably oak, and without mast or sail, this was no vessel for ocean voyages or rough seas. But it served well enough to carry the invaders southwards close to the shore until they reached the Straits of Dover, where the coast of Britain lay within sight and easy reach. Once across the straits, the longboat was ideal for nosing up the tidal creeks and narrow waterways of East Anglia. It was rowed by fourteen pairs of oarsmen, so that, with the steersman, and a few others, the boat could carry 30 to 40 warriors, but there was little room for stores or equipment and none at all for women and children.

The map below shows the routes of the invaders who fell upon Britain when the Romans had gone. While the Teutonic warriors made for the east coast, the Picts and Scots ravaged the north.

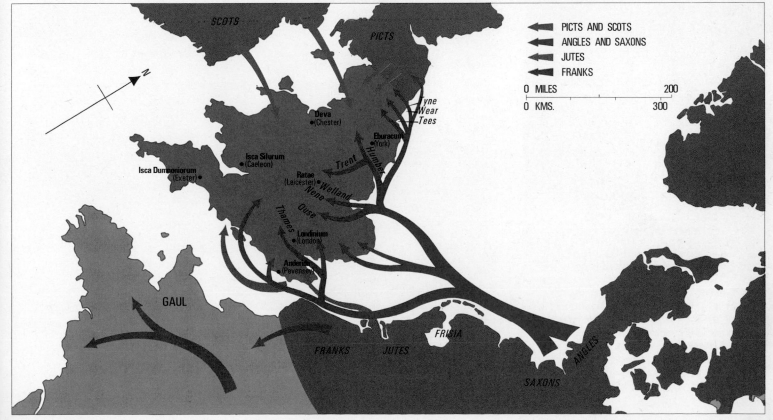

The Saxons Settle

When the last of the Roman legions departed, Britain was not suddenly flooded by waves of savage invaders. For a time, life went on in much the same way; gradually, however, as trade died away and law and order faded, people heard stories of more landings along the coast. This was nothing new. The pirates had been raiding for 200 years but, now, instead of stealing a few slaves and cattle, they were making homes for themselves on the low land by the rivers. Why did they come to live in a foreign land? In their homeland, much of the soil was poor and thin, with farms too small to support a race of warriors, so the young men went raiding and brought the booty home. Yet they longed for land of their own to plough. Other peoples were pressing in from the east, so the Angles and Saxons took to their boats and made their way to Britain. The disciplined legions had gone, the coastal forts were empty and no squadrons of war galleys patrolled the river-mouths. Here was land in plenty and no-one to drive them off. All down the east coast they could land where they pleased. The invaders decided to stay.

This Pictish stone cross, with its delightful deer, sea-horses and strange Loch Ness-type monster, is an emblem of the earliest days of Christianity in Britain. St Ninian was converting the heathen beyond the Wall in Galloway from 397 to 432, the year in which St Patrick returned to Ireland. The pagan Saxons wiped out Christianity in much of the country but the faith lived on in the West and in parts of the North.

The cruel fighters

The settlers came in small numbers. We read of three ships coming to Kent, of two chiefs appearing in a river mouth with five ships. That would have meant 100 newcomers in one place and perhaps 200 further along the coast—all of them young fighting-men. The Saxons, who got their name from their favourite weapon, the *seax*, a short one-handed sword, were known to be the cruellest of all the tribes. Each band followed its war-lord and were eager to fight and to die, if they must, when he died in battle. They brought no women or old men, and they moved about easily, using the rivers to carry them inland. Sometimes, the groups would join together under one leader—a *bretwalda* or overlord.

Compare this old "map" of the Saxon Shore forts with one on page 22. Left to right, from the top, these are: Orthona (Bradwell), Dubris (Dover), Lemanis (Lympne), Branodunum (Brancaster), Gariannonum (Burgh), Regulbium (Reculver), Rutupiae (Richborough), Anderida (Pevensey), and Portus Adurni (Porchester).

Saxons looting London. The once-thriving city lay in ruins for some 400 years.

28

Anglo-Saxon homes

By 500, there were dozens of settlements in East Anglia, the midlands and the south. Usually, it was easy enough to defeat the Britons; there was no need to kill them all, only to take some for wives and a few perhaps for cowherds and labourers; the rest could escape to the west or into the hills. Some of the Britons lived as refugees amid the ruins of the towns, for the Anglo-Saxons avoided those places.

They did not understand how to build in brick and stone, nor how to use stoves, baths, theatres and churches. In any case, Britain was not like Gaul; the Roman ways had not gone very deep and once the architects, officials and merchants had gone, the Britons could not run the towns. They forgot Latin, and took more easily to Anglo-Saxon words.

The green mounds and jagged walls (above, left) are part of the defences of Richborough, the first of the Saxon Shore forts. Doubtless, the Britons held it until overwhelmed by the enemy, but the Saxon invaders do not seem to have used elaborate forts of this kind. The picture (above, right) shows a section of the outer wall, which was added later.

The warriors become kings

When the warriors had seized a patch of the country, they built themselves a thatched timber hall in which to sleep and feast as companions should; they added a few huts, bowers and barns, protecting them all by a ditch and a fence of hewn logs. As one *bretwalda* or overlord became stronger than the other chiefs in the district, these crude settlements merged together into small kingdoms, like Essex and Deira in the north; the *bretwalda* became the king, his best warriors and closest followers became nobles. The spoils of war were soon used up, and a king wishing to reward his followers gave them grants of land. Thus the land, at first held in common, increasingly became private property. Men who were feeble, timid or dull-witted fell to the level of serfs, with the captives taken in battle. So the rough equality of Saxon warriors living and fighting together changed to a system of king, nobles, fighting-men and lowly serfs.

The picture shows a Saxon ox-drawn plough. The English newcomers avoided the forests and the chalk uplands because they were lowlanders and cattle farmers, so they settled in river valleys where they found pasture and open fields for their heavy ploughs. They liked stiff clay soil and gradually felled stretches of woodland to grow wheat for bread and barley from which they brewed ale. They loved feasting and were famous for the amount of meat they ate and of the ale they drank.

The Legend of Arthur

Who was King Arthur? Did he ever exist or was he just a romantic figure in a mass of legends which have been handed down through the ages? These legends had been told and retold for centuries when, in 1469, Thomas Malory wrote them down to please Edward IV.

According to legend, Arthur, the son of King Uther Pendragon, was brought up in secrecy by the wizard Merlin. Years later, the boy proved himself the rightful king when he alone was able to pull a sword out of a block of stone. With his magic sword, Excalibur, Arthur conquered many countries and, at his Court in the city of Camelot, he was served by a company of knights—Lancelot, Kaye, Gawain, Galahad and many others. They dined at a huge Round Table and often rode away to carry out noble deeds. The reign ended in tragedy when quarrelling broke out among the knights and Arthur himself was mortally wounded. He was laid in a barge which carried him away to the fabulous Isle of Avalon, from which he would return if ever his people were in dire peril.

Here is a bronze statue of King Arthur, made at Innsbruck by Peter Vischer, a 16th-century German sculptor, who gave him the armour of his own time. This is King Arthur of the story books and romantic fables.

The Britons' hero

What are the facts about King Arthur? We have nothing that was written in the sixth century when he is supposed to have lived—only some poems and legends about a mighty hero who drove back the Anglo-Saxon invaders, and also some old copies of still older writings. One document tells of the "strife of Camlann", in 539, when Arthur perished, and the great Battle of Badon in which Arthur and the Britons were victorious. The monk Gildas writes about this battle but does not mention Arthur, though a ninth century writer, Nennius, speaks of him as the "battle leader" who commanded the armies of all the kings of Britain. He also lists a dozen battles which Arthur won, but no one has located more than one or two of the places. Some people claim that Arthur's realm was in Cumberland, others say in Wales, and a great many others believe that Camelot was in Cornwall or in the West Country. Archaeologists have recently excavated an old camp, Cadbury Castle, in Somerset, which has many claims to be the original Camelot. What does seem clear is that around the year 500, a leader of the Britons defeated the invaders several times and so became a hero whose deeds lived on in legend.

Could Arthur have resembled this Celtic warrior? This is in fact a picture of Taranis, a Celtic god, "The Thunderer" or the Jupiter of his people. The portrait shows clearly the personal armour of the time—an embossed shield, helmet (worn as a rule only by chiefs) and tough leather jerkin; chainmail was very rare in the 6th century and plate armour, like that in the picture opposite, was totally unknown.

A knight takes leave of Arthur and Queen Guinevere.

Arthur rides out with his knights.

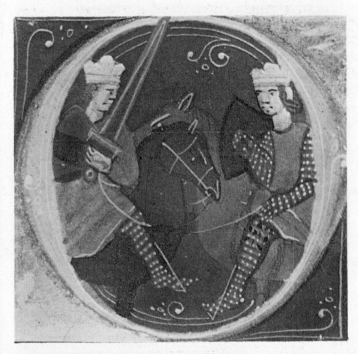
Arthur ambushed by an enemy king.

Arthur slays a king (or perhaps Mordred).

Medieval picture of Arthur on a ship, surrounded by knights.

Arthur and Guinevere

These lively pictures from medieval romances show scenes from a few of the legends which surround Arthur's name. One version of the story tells how Guinevere, a most beautiful princess, was escorted to her marriage by Sir Lancelot, who fell secretly in love with her and she with him. Nevertheless, to please her father, she married Arthur. Mordred was jealous of Lancelot and put round a story that he and Guinevere had been false to the king; she was condemned to death but Lancelot galloped up and carried her away to safety. She was restored to Court but he was exiled for killing Sir Gareth. Meanwhile, Mordred raised a rebellion and although Arthur slew him in combat, he himself was mortally wounded. Knowing this, he told Sir Bedivere to throw his sword Excalibur into a lake; twice he disobeyed but on the third occasion an arm rose from the water, caught the sword and drew it beneath the waves. Arthur was then carried to a waiting barge, which took him to the magic Isle of Avalon.

The Dark Ages

For about 200 years (A.D. 400–600), the history of Britain is almost blank. We know next to nothing about what happened, about the people, who they were, how they lived, fought and died. That is why this period is called the Dark Ages.

We do not know, for instance, how Arthur fought the Anglo-Saxons. Was he the last Roman-style general, commanding disciplined troops like the Roman legions? Or did his men fight the invaders in the same wild manner as Boadicea's troops had fought? The picture on the opposite page shows three of Arthur's knights mounted and armed like Norman barons, but we can be fairly sure that the real Arthur had no chainmail, stirrups or heavy cavalry horses. Probably he and his men rode about the country attacking the Saxon foot soldiers in an open, mobile style of warfare; battles would have been fought mainly at river-crossings and the numbers involved would probably have been no more than a thousand warriors a side.

It seems likely that Arthur drove the invaders out of the south Midlands and kept up the struggle for several years, but his triumphs did not last.

Dozmary Pool, Cornwall—is Excalibur in its waters?

Could Camelot have been here, at Tintagel Castle?

Where was Camelot?

Arthur's kingdom—if indeed he was a king—is generally supposed to have been somewhere in the West Country. The legend of Camelot is strongest there, yet his name haunts places all over Britain. Dozmary Pool is said to have been the lake into which Sir Bedivere threw the sword Excalibur when Arthur lay dying. Yet some experts say that his last battle of Camlann took place near Hadrian's Wall, hundreds of miles from Cornwall.

There have long been links be-tween Arthur's name and Glaston-bury in Somerset; British forts have been unearthed in the area. Although Tintagel in Cornwall lies in what could have been a western kingdom, the castle itself is Norman and could not possibly have been used by Arthur. Welsh legend and poetry place Camelot in Wales, perhaps at Caerleon, while Malory himself set Arthur's capital at Winchester.

Many people believe that excavations which the Camelot Research Committee began in 1966 will prove that Arthur's stronghold was situated at South Cadbury in Somerset. The great Iron-Age hill-fort was occupied in the fifth–sixth century when a large timbered hall was built. While this may have been the headquarters of a powerful leader, there are, so far, no traces of a "many-towered" city. Other places far from the West Country have connections with Arthur, such as Dover, Carlisle, Edinburgh and Liddesdale in Scotland, and even the Orkneys, lying north of the mainland.

The Round Table

The Round Table in the Great Hall at Winchester.

Malory tells how, as a wedding gift from Queen Guinevere's father, Arthur received a Round Table at which his knights might sit in equal fellowship. None would feel that he sat either above or below his companions. When Malory's book came to be printed, Caxton wrote that the Round Table could be seen at Winchester and this, for many years, was believed to be Arthur's own table. However, the round table which now hangs in the hall of Winchester Castle was made for Henry III in the thirteenth century. It measures about five metres across, is made of oak and bears round its edge the names of some of the most famous knights. They include Sir Kaye, the King's foster-brother, Sir Mordred the traitor, Sir Lance-lot whose love for Queen Guinevere broke up the fellowship and Sir Galahad, the noble young knight who found the Holy Grail. This, the cup which Christ used at the Last Supper, was seen in a vision by the knights as they sat at table; some vowed to set out in search of it; they met with many adventures and some returned to Camelot, but Sir Galahad never came back. He discovered the Grail in a far-off land and died soon afterwards.

There was no higher honour in the land than to be one of the Knights of the Round Table, and anyone who was oppressed by a tyrant or a witch could send to King Arthur for help. One or more of his Knights would ride to the rescue.

This oak carving in the House of Lords shows Sir Galahad riding out on the Quest of the Holy Grail with Sir Bors and Sir Percival.

The Seven Kingdoms

As the Angles and Saxons advanced, driving the Britons into the west, a number of small kingdoms arose. The first ones were Kent, Essex, East Anglia and, in the north, two whose names have vanished—Deira and Bernicia. Presently, Northumbria, Mercia and Wessex came to the fore. As there were usually about seven of these kingdoms, this period is called the Heptarchy, from the Greek word, *hepta* = seven.

Fighting was always going on, boundaries changed and the little kingdoms rose and fell, according to the warlike ability of the king. If he was slain in battle and the heir was a child, then the kingdom would be beset by enemies.

Often, the strongest king would be recognised by the others as *bretwalda* or overlord. They would bring their men to fight under his banner and would grant him certain rights. They would, for instance, give safe passage to any of his people—when, in 625, the King of Kent's sister rode north to marry Edwin of Northumbria, his vassals the East Angles and the Middle Angles, escorted her through their territory to the border of his realm.

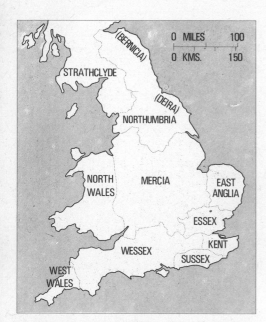

Leaving out Strathclyde, North Wales and West Wales, which were inhabited by Celtic tribesmen and Britons, you can see that the Saxon Kingdoms numbered seven—Sussex, Kent, Essex, East Anglia, Northumbria, Mercia and Wessex. In the 6th century, Kent was the richest and most advanced of the new kingdoms, then Northumbria became supreme in the 7th century, with three famous kings—Edwin, Oswald and Oswy. Penda of Mercia reduced Northumbria's power and, in the 8th century, it was Mercia's turn to take the lead. Lastly, Wessex arose, when Egbert defeated the Mercians at the battle of Ellandune in 825, and this caused the other kingdoms to acknowledge him as their overlord. He is generally considered to be the first real king of England, and he was the grandfather of Alfred the Great.

This coin bears the portrait and name of Offa, King of Mercia, 757 to 796.

The rival monarchs

The first important king was Ethelred of Kent (d. 616) and, after him, Edwin of Northumbria. He and his successor, the saintly Oswald, were both slain in battle by Penda of Mercia, a ferocious old pagan who dominated the scene for thirty years and killed off most of the rival monarchs. Mercia stayed supreme in the eighth century because, in Ethelbald and Offa, it had two strong kings who ruled for many years. Offa was all-powerful in the south and the midlands; Charlemagne, the greatest man in Europe, regarded him as "King of Britain". They exchanged gifts, made a treaty and considered joining their families by a royal marriage.

Edwin of Northumbria married Ethelburga, sister of the King of Kent. She and her priest Paulinus had converted him and his subjects to Christianity, when the kingdom was attacked by Cadwallor of Wales and Penda. Edwin was killed in battle in 632.

WODEN

KENT	WESSEX	BERNICIA	DEIRA	MERCIA
Wecta	Baeldaeg		Waegdeg	Wihtlaeg
	Brand		Sigegar	Waermund
			Swefdaeg	Offa
	Freothogar	Benoc	Sigegeat	Angeltheof
Witta	Freawine	Aloc	Saebald	Eomaer
			Saefugel	Icel
	Wig	Angenwit	Westerfalca	Cnebba
	Gewis	Ingui	Wilgils	Cynewold
Wihtgils	Esla	Esa	Uscfrea	Creoda
	Elesa	Eoppa	Yffe	Pybba
Hengist	Cerdic	Ida	Aelle	Penda

NORTHUMBRIA

Ethelbert
Saebehrt
(nephew)

EAST SAXONS

To strengthen their position and increase the people's respect, kings claimed to be descended from the god Woden. Here you can see how the Anglo-Saxon chronicle traced the ancestry of 5 kings back through mythical heroes to the father god.

A Land of Saints and Scholars

As the pagan conquerors spread across the land, they wiped out almost every trace of the Christian religion which had flourished in Roman times. In Wales and in the extreme south-west, the Church survived, though the hard-pressed Christians seem to have made no attempt to convert the heathen newcomers. Perhaps some of them tried and perished horribly. However, it was from Wales that Christianity reached Ireland, Scotland and the North of England, for Saint Patrick was a Roman Briton brought up by Christian parents in Glamorgan or the Severn Valley during the last years of Roman rule. He was to spend most of his life in Ireland, breaking the power of the Druids and converting the Irish to Christianity. Born half a century after Patrick's death, Saint Columba set out from Northern Ireland to found the famous monastery at Iona. Irish monks carried the word of God through the land of the heathen Picts and Saint Aidan travelled from Iona to Northumbria where he built a monastery on the island of Lindisfarne. The Irish saints—Patrick, Columba and Aidan—founded the Celtic Church at a time when most of England lay in darkness.

An Irish monastery would consist of little more than a few "beehive" cells like this one in County Kerry.

Giving up everything

Irish monks lived lives of absolute poverty and simplicity; they owned nothing and they ate, drank and spoke as little as possible. Although monks lived together and followed a set of rules, any monk could live a solitary life in the community or he might go to some lonelier place, perhaps to live like Saint Cuthbert in a hole in the ground on the tiny island of Farne. This idea of giving up everything for a life of prayer was looked upon with the greatest respect and admiration, and when Saint Cuthbert's fellow-monks gently drew him back into the world to become Bishop of Lindisfarne, they did so with reluctance. The hermit's life was the highest form of dedication to God.

A great saint

Saint Patrick (b. about 385) was the son of a Roman official who lived in Wales or the West of England. Seized by Irish pirates who were raiding the district, Patrick was sold to an Irish chieftain who made him a cowherd. After six years, the lad escaped and made his way to Gaul to study for the priesthood. Later, the Pope sent him to Ireland as a missionary and there, in not much more than ten years of ceaseless travelling and preaching, he turned Ireland into a Christian country. In his "Confessions", he wrote, "Christ the Lord . . . bade me come here and stay for the rest of my life".

A page from the Lindisfarne Gospel, showing the wonderful 7th-century lettering. These Gospels had covers decorated with gold and jewels.

A marvel of history

One of the marvels of history is the way in which art and learning flourished in the north of England during the seventh and eighth centuries. At a time when life was crude and harsh, when barely one man in a thousand could read or write, monks of the Celtic Church were producing most beautifully written and illustrated books. They worked in tiny unheated cells, joyfully accepting a total lack of comfort, because their books were for the glory of God and the Christian religion. They wrote and taught in Latin in order to pass on knowledge, stories and accounts of daily happenings. Some monks spent their lives making copies of the Gospels, for there was no way to produce a book, except by hand.

Saint Patrick, in bishop's robes.

On the right, you can see the remains of a Celtic cross and behind it one of the bee-hive-shaped cells which can be seen on Skellig Michael, a small island lying 8 miles off the coast of Ireland. Celtic monks founded a monastery there in the 6th or 7th century, when it was quite common for devout Christians to seek out some remote place in which to live a hermit-like life of prayer and meditation.

The Treasure of Sutton Hoo

The most splendid treasure ever discovered anywhere in the Western world was found in 1939 at Sutton Hoo, in Suffolk. An East Saxon burial ship had already been unearthed when traces of another ship were found in a large mound. The excavators located a burial chamber still intact in the centre of this ship and, on opening it, uncovered an astounding hoard of armour, bowls, ornaments, spoons, dishes, an iron standard, a huge whetstone and many other objects. But there was no body, no crown, no proof that the missing warrior was a king. Whoever he was, he was certainly a chieftain of great wealth, for his treasures came from all over the known world—spoons and bowls from Constantinople and Egypt, helmet, shield and sword from Sweden, clasps, harness buckles and the lid of his purse from the workshop of some Saxon master-jeweller, for they were blazing with gold, enamels and gems. The coins in his purse came from Gaul and these show that the burial took place in about 650–660. Was the dead hero lost at sea or in a flood? Was he buried somewhere else, perhaps in a Christian grave?

Who was the hero of Sutton Hoo?

Every Saxon king and chief had his band of followers who dwelt with him in his timber hall. His power depended upon his ability to lead them successfully in war and to reward them with food, drink and princely gifts. When he died, his son did not automatically take his place, for the warriors would not wish to be led by a weakling or a child. The elders might choose his brother, a nephew or perhaps some relative who had proved himself in battle. If the missing hero of Sutton Hoo was a king of the East Angles, he might have been one of two who died in 654. King Ethelhere is said to have perished in battle in the north of England; suppose, for some reason, his body was never recovered, might not his pagan followers have prepared a shipload of precious things which he would be sure to need in the next world?

A medieval artist's idea of King David (right), monarch and lawgiver. We do not know if the early Saxon kings wore crowns.

The longship of Sutton Hoo (far right) being excavated in 1939. The timbers had rotted away but you can see their outline and the iron bolts.

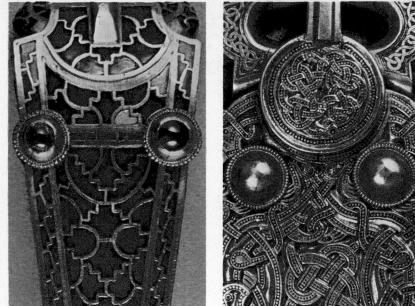

Some of the Sutton Hoo treasures: (left to right) a gold and enamel buckle; an enamelled disc on a bowl; a buckle with jewels; the great belt buckle, 5 inches long, solid gold and perhaps the finest article in the treasure hoard.

Saxon sword-blades and shorter one-handed scramasaxes. These are 8th-century weapons.

How Saxons fought ...

The Saxon warrior fought with sword, spear and round shield. Some carried battle-axes but by no means all of them wore helmets. Body armour was no more than a leather jerkin, perhaps with some metal rings sewn on it for extra protection. Though the Saxons often rode to battle, they preferred to fight on foot.

how they farmed ...

Saxons were farmers as well as fighters. They brought heavy ploughs with them and so were able to cultivate clay soils as well as lighter land. They grew wheat, barley, rye and oats, kept cattle for meat and sheep for the wool needed to weave cloth. Both men and women loved jewellery and bright colours.

how they lived

At home, the Saxons were barbarians compared with Romano-Britons. A king's "palace" was a smoke-filled timber hall with thatched roof and mud floor; a "banquet" was an endless supply of meat, bread and ale. Their music was the gleeman's harp and song, their literature, a poem of battles, monsters and terrible gods.

Two Rival Churches

As we have seen, Christianity reached Britain in Roman times but was driven into Wales by the heathen Anglo-Saxons. There the faith survived, while St Patrick carried the Gospel to Ireland. The Irish Church soon produced scholars and missionaries and it was St Columba who journeyed to Iona to convert the Picts.

But the Celtic Church, cut off from the continent, developed in its own way and this was different from the Church of Rome which now ruled much of Europe. So, in 597, Pope Gregory, anxious to unite all Christians, sent St Augustine to Britain, where he converted the kingdom of Kent but failed to make friends with the British Christians of Wales. Next, St Paulinus went north to convert the Northumbrians, but when Penda slew King Edwin, he fled back to Kent. Christianity in the north was saved by St Aidan who came from Iona to spread the influence of the Celtic Church. However, at the Synod (Council) of Whitby in 663, King Oswy decided that Northumbria should be part of the Church of Rome. In time, the Welsh and the Irish agreed with this step and the whole Church was united to Rome.

This old engraving shows St Birinus, a courageous priest of Gaul who journeyed to England, preaching to the heathen West Saxons.

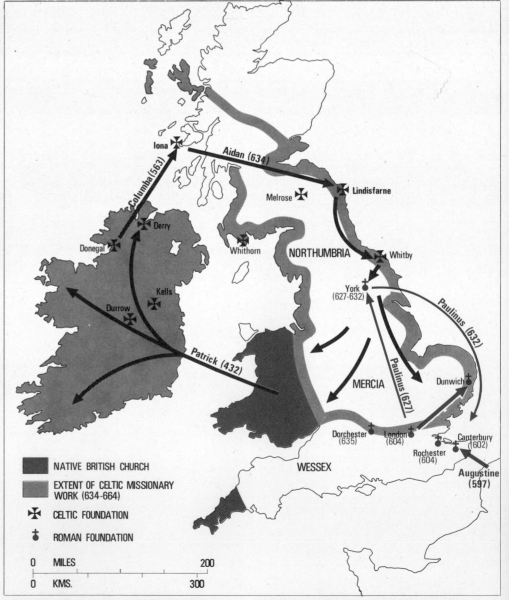

NATIVE BRITISH CHURCH

EXTENT OF CELTIC MISSIONARY WORK (634-664)

✠ CELTIC FOUNDATION

♱ ROMAN FOUNDATION

The map shows how Christianity spread into Ireland, Northumbria and Mercia, and also from Kent. When the Synod of Whitby took place, the influence of the Celtic Church was much more widespread than Rome's.

King Ecgfrith (above) begs St Cuthbert to become bishop.

Whitby Abbey (above), where King Oswy of Northumbria presided over the Synod of Whitby, 663. Bishops and clergy came from all over Britain and, after earnest discussion, the majority agreed to accept the Roman date for Easter and the rule of the Pope. The turning-point came, apparently, when the pious Oswy asked if it were true that St Peter had been given the keys of heaven; the clergy from Iona and Rome all agreed that this was true. In that case, declared Oswy, he would obey St Peter—and Rome.

Mission to the English

St Augustine's mission to the English in 597 was no haphazard venture. It was a planned operation in which the chances of success were high. Ethelbert, King of Kent, had married a Frankish princess who was a Christian and so, while he himself still worshipped Woden and Thor, he was quite cordial to the missionaries. He also realised that they could extend his power when he and his people accepted Christianity. Augustine next made contact with the Christians in the West and went to meet them at a place in the Severn Valley. The Welsh bishops were suspicious but they agreed to listen to the stranger if he showed them friendship and respect; Augustine, however, was tactless and did not rise to greet them nor did he hesitate to tell them to accept the Pope's authority. The Welsh withdrew indignantly and Augustine returned to Kent. He had little success outside the county but, in the north of England, Aidan and Cuthbert, saints of the Celtic Church, made much wider progress in their missionary work. St Cuthbert was specially loved as the patron saint of Northumbria.

St Augustine in the Archbishop's seat: after his failure in Wales, he devoted his life to Kent and died there in about 605. He was buried in the monastery which he and the monks from Rome founded in Canterbury.

The Literate Few

Until Alfred's time, few kings and nobles bothered with learning. The arts of reading and writing were left to monks and scribes, which was natural enough because since Roman days the Church had to educate boys for the priesthood. This work was interrupted by the heathen invaders, but Ireland escaped and Irish missionaries carried learning to Scotland and Northumbria. The monasteries at Jarrow, Wearmouth and York became so famous for their schools and libraries that pupils came to them from all over Europe.

Meanwhile, the Angles and Saxons began to produce scholars and writers; well-known schools were founded at Canterbury, Dunwich and Malmesbury but none could equal the fame of the Northumbrian monasteries. It was there that Bede wrote books and a history of the Church; it was there that an unknown monk wrote down the epic poem "Beowulf" which minstrels had been singing for 200 years or more. In the ninth century Viking invasions almost wiped out all this learning but Alfred did his utmost to restore the schools and in his reign the Anglo-Saxon Chronicle was started.

Part of a page from The Anglo-Saxon Chronicle. It tells of a battle at Brunanburgh in 937.

A page from an illustrated Grammar Book, written about 990 by Aelfric for boys in monastic schools.

The Anglo-Saxon Chronicle

This is a history book, the oldest in Europe to be written in the language of its country. It was started in 890 in King Alfred's reign, when a Wessex writer had the idea of setting down a continuous history of his people. For the distant past, he turned to poems and stories about old kings and their battles, but he also had Bede's writings, one or two lists of kings and some brief notes which monks had written on the margins of their books. For events of his own time, such as the coming of the Norsemen, he could rely on eye-witnesss accounts.

It has been thought that Alfred himself may have started the Chronicle, but it is more likely that he encouraged the writer and read his work.

Soon after 890, copies of the original Chronicle were being passed round various monasteries; one copy went up to York where someone added a few notes about Northumbrian history. In other monasteries, such as Winchester, the Chronicle was kept up to date right to the Norman Conquest and, at Peterborough, as far as Stephen's reign. The chronicler ends with a vivid picture of the miseries of civil war: "Then was corn dear, and flesh and cheese and butter; for there was none in the land. Wretched men died of hunger. . . . If two or three men came riding into a town, all the township fled before them, imagining them to be robbers."

From "Beowulf"—an Old English poem full of heroes, monsters and pure poetry, like this description of a sea-crossing:

Away she went over a wavy ocean,
boat like a bird, breaking seas,
wind-whetted, white-throated,
till curved prow had ploughed so far—
the sun standing right on the second day—
that they might see land loom on the sky line
then the shimmer of cliffs, sheer moors behind,
reaching capes. The crossing was at an end.

© Michael Alexander.
[Penguin Books Ltd]

A great scholar
In 680 the Venerable Bede, left, ("venerable" meant "worthy of love") was taken into the twin-monastery of Wearmouth–Jarrow as a small orphan. Under a kindly abbot, the boy grew up to become one of the greatest scholars in Europe. His books covered every branch of knowledge in his day— the Bible, science, grammar, astronomy and rhetoric. But it is his "Ecclesiastical History of Britain" which provides so much of our knowledge of early Saxon times. Monks sent him information from all over the kingdom but it was Bede, writing in his cell at Jarrow, who wove these accounts into what is our first great history.

The Coming of the Vikings

It was in 793, in Offa's reign, that the Vikings first struck at the English kingdoms. A fleet appeared off the holy island of Lindisfarne and a band of robbers came ashore to smash their way into St Cuthbert's church, to slaughter the monks and to sail gleefully away with the treasures of gold and silver piled into their long dragon-ships. Who were these Vikings, where did they come from and why?

Known also as Norsemen, Danes and Northmen, the Vikings were Scandinavian farmers from the bleak lands of northern Europe. Suddenly—perhaps because of bad harvests or because of a sudden rise in the birth-rate, the young men took to going "i-viking", i.e. raiding in the summer months. A band of them would set out in long-ships and sail along the coast of France across the sea to Britain to attack towns, villages and, above all, monasteries filled with the wealth of generations. To strike terror was their stock-in-trade. They robbed, burnt and killed in a cold fury, savaging every coast of Europe. Then they would go home to spend the winter feasting and boasting of their exploits against the soft peoples of the southerly lands.

Carved horse's head from the long-ship which was unearthed from a mound at Gokstad in Norway in 1880. The Vikings loved horses and were expert riders; when raiding, they made a point of going ashore to steal horses so that they could make plundering forays across the country-side.

This picture from a 12th century bible shows Norsemen attacking an English town. The artist has given them shields and helmets like those which the Normans wore at Hastings. This was not absurd, because the Viking attacks fall into two periods, (i) about 800 to 875 and (ii) 975 to 1016—only 50 years before the Conquest.

The Viking bases

Each long-ship carried a crew of perhaps eighty fighting-men and, in the early days of raiding, they would attack monasteries on the northern coasts. Surprise was all-important, for, when it failed, as at Jarrow, the English would bring up superior forces. Soon the Vikings seized islands in the Orkneys and Hebrides and used them as jumping-off bases for further raids to the south and to Ireland. Next, they gave up hit-and-run raids and began to organise armies of conquest. In 836 they had a colony at Dublin and three years later Thorgils set himself up as the first of the sea-kings of Ireland. By the 850s and '60s, the Viking host was spending the winter in southern England, secure behind the stockades of well-provisioned forts. Then the "Great Army" would resume fighting in the spring. By now, they wanted land on which to settle but, thanks to King Alfred, they did not completely conquer England.

The sea-robbers took to regular warfare with the sort of thoroughness used in training modern commandos and paratroops. At home, they trained for the fighting season in special camps like the one below, which has been reconstructed at Trelleborg in Denmark. A timber house for the warriors can be seen through the fortress gateway. Land shortage and a rising population caused this explosion of Viking fury.

Where they settled

The map below shows the pattern of settlement by the Viking pirates-turned-conquerors. Starting with raids on Jarrow and Wearmouth, they launched full-scale invasions in the ninth century, settling first around York and then penetrating the Midlands and East Anglia. Triangles show the winter bases of the Great Army; the shaded portions are lands occupied by the Vikings; "flames" show where major battles were fought. Alfred's Wessex lay immediately south of the occupied territory.

Eventually, the Vikings settled down to farming and not all the victories of Alfred and his sons could turn them off the lands they had seized.

This early Viking long-ship was sturdy enough to cross the North Sea, yet its draught was shallow enough for it to be rowed up narrow rivers. She was clinker-built (having overlapping planks) with 16 strakes, or planks a side, all made with oak and fastened with iron nails and bolts. Her mast, ingeniously supported on a solid block to avoid straining the light craft, carried a large square sail which would be lowered when approaching land to make the vessel less likely to be seen. The ship was rowed by thirty-two oars, which passed through circular rowlocks cut in the side. Her rudder, shaped like an oar, was fastened to the right-hand (steerboard) side. The skin-covered chests served as rowing benches and contained the crew's food rations, weapons and loot; their round shields were hung along the sides. The crew numbered about 50 but there was space for another 20 or 30 warriors. These men were carefully chosen, for a man had to be as good at an oar as with a sword; all were volunteers between 16 and 60; all were equal under the captain and all shared the plunder, which was divided according to custom.

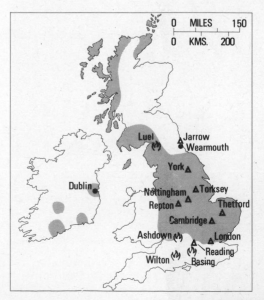

The Viking Epic

GREENLAND

ICELAND

Faroe Islands

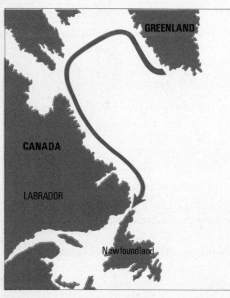

GREENLAND

CANADA

LABRADOR

Newfoundland

This map shows the Vikings' probable route to Vinland (North America).

A strikingly similar coastline (above) shown on an old Viking map.

Iona

IRELAND

Dublin

Carved head showing the conical helmet with nose-piece worn by the later Vikings.

ASTURIAS

EMIRATE OF COR

Lisbon

Cadiz

The Viking epic

On the map the Vikings' homelands are shown in red, and you can see how their dragon-ships carried them plundering and settling all over Western Europe and far beyond. If you follow the red arrows, you will see that the Danes sailed mainly to England and France, and that the Norwegians made for Scotland and Ireland, besides founding colonies in Iceland and Greenland and actually reaching North America. Some Vikings attacked the coastal cities of Spain and entered the Mediterranean, while the Swedes made immense journeys down the rivers of Eastern Europe into Russia and on to the Black Sea and Constantinople, which they called "Micklegard".

LAPPS

Volga

Staraya Ladoga

Volkhov

Novgorod

CASPIAN
SEA

NORWAY

Birka

SWEDEN

Dvina

tland
ands

Islands

Neman

rne

DENMARK

Kiev   Dnieper

SLAVS

Rhine

Meuse

MAGYARS

BLACK SEA

Seine   Paris

HOLY ROMAN EMPIRE

Rhône

BULGARS

Constantinople

aronne

Luna
Pisa

BYZANTINE   EMPIRE

Corsica

Sardinia

Sicily

MEDITERRANEAN   SEA

ATE OF MAGHRIB

The Sea Wolves

In all history, there have been no people—Goths, Vandals, Huns included—who have been more dreaded than the Vikings. These sea-pirates were more deliberately brutal, greedy and cruel than any other invaders who have reached Britain's shores, and for more than 200 years they terrorised not merely the coastal fringes but the entire country. By the middle of the ninth century, fleets of two and three hundred vessels were arriving every year, and hordes of bloodthirsty warriors spread across the land forming themselves into the "heathen host" as the Saxons called their Great Army. Before long, they were building fortified camps and staying the winter, in order to resume plundering in the spring. When they saw that there was no need to go home, they sent for their wives and children to come and settle in a land that was greener and more fertile than their own. At heart, these ruffians were farmers and traders and, for all their vices, they possessed energy, courage and brotherly loyalty to one another. In their pride in themselves, they mixed very little with the vanquished Saxons, but followed their own laws and customs and worshipped their own gods.

Stern of the Oseberg ship discovered in 1904. Clay had preserved its oak timbers and it now stands in a Norwegian museum. Strangely, the rudder is on the left (port) side, instead of on the right (starboard) side.

Ancestors of the kings of England

The Viking attacks fell not only upon England. All the coasts of Europe felt their lash, especially those of France. Paris, Rouen, Nantes and scores of other towns were burnt and pillaged and it was in France that the Vikings first demanded blackmail money, the famous *Danegeld*, to go away—after which they presently returned for more.

The river Seine was a natural highway and the Vikings made full use of it to plunder the French countryside. In 912 Rollo or Rolf secured from Charles the Simple a district of France, later known as Normandy. In return, Rollo agreed to become Charles' vassal and to accept Christianity. He was bap-

An artist's version of the seizure of Normandy in 911 by Rollo, the Danish leader. The Vikings were much more likely to have sailed up the River Seine than to have landed on this rocky coast.

tised in Rouen and ruled his dukedom justly for a number of years.

Rollo was the ancestor of William the Conqueror and therefore of the later kings of England.

The Viking gods

Not surprisingly, the Viking gods were as pitiless as their human worshippers. Odin (Woden) gave gifts, such as courage, victory and wisdom, but, in the end, he always played false and when he chose to award defeat, he would take no notice of prayers and sacrifices. Yet, men accepted death in order to go to Odin's realm, there to enjoy eternal battle and unending feasting in his hall, Valhalla.

Thor, the red-bearded god with burning eyes, made thunder when he clattered about the sky in his goat-drawn wagon; lightning was the flash of his axe-hammer, Miolnir, as he hurled it against the giants and trolls. Njord and his twin children, Freyr and Freya, gave good harvests and healthy children.

A bronze plaque (above) showing Odin with a wolf-headed figure. Unlike Christianity, Viking religion was ultimately hopeless, morbid and cruel; there would be no happiness, only doom, when Fenris, the wolf, got free and devoured Odin at Ragnarok, the final disaster for gods and men.

A Valkyrie, one of Odin's servants who rode about on his errands, escorting dead warriors to Valhalla and often bringing disaster. Sometimes they took the form of beautiful maidens who inspired young men and brought them victory.

A 10th-century Icelandic carving, only 6 cm high, of the god Thor. The terrible red-bearded Thunderer seems to be in a benevolent mood.

The Viking Colonies in the West

Instead of making for the richer lands to the south, some of the Vikings from Norway sailed westward to Iceland and Greenland. Iceland was discovered in about 870, probably by voyagers blown off course. A colony was founded which became a free state, governed by an *althing* or parliament. This unusual state of affairs was probably due to the fact that there was no-one there to fight or to rob. Greenland was discovered in 984 by Erik the Red, a tough aggressive character who had been banished from Norway to Iceland for killing a man. Accused of another murder in Iceland, Erik was exiled for three years, so he sailed west and came to a land partly covered with grass, bushes and trees which he named Greenland. When the three years were up, he returned to Iceland to recruit settlers and was soon off again with a fleet of 25 ships (11 never arrived) carrying men, women, food, cattle and furnishings to the new country. The settlers built homes of turf and stones and soon got their farms going. Greenland was to prove the jumping-off place for America. And Eric the Red's son was to be the first to set foot there.

The Oseberg ship (right) as she was before reconstruction. She was 71 feet long, a vessel large enough for most ventures, but the ships that made the voyages to North America were stouter, with higher sides.

A superb example (above) of ship-building skill—the 9th-century ship found at Gokstad in Norway. A peacock's skull found on board suggests that the owner had been to Western Europe where peacocks were much prized at the courts of Frankish rulers.

Sailing to America

Two stories were written at an early date about the discovery of America, one in Greenland (the Flatey Book) and one in Iceland (Hank's Book). According to them, the first man to set eyes on the American coast was Biarni, a young man whose father was a neighbour of Erik the Red. Biarni had been trading in Norway and, in making for home, he and his men became lost in fog and passed the southern-most tip of Greenland. They sailed on and sighted a level wooded land which may have been Newfoundland: then they turned northwards along the coast and eventually reached Greenland without having actually landed anywhere.

Biarni seems to have been teased for being so timid; however, he may have inspired Leif Eriksson, son of Erik the Red, to provision a ship and to set sail for the west in 1002. The first land he came to was so barren, he called it Helluland (slateland) but, turning south, he found more pleasant country which he named Markland (forest land). This was Labrador or, possibly, Nova Scotia. Two more days and nights brought Leif and his men to an island where they went ashore, built houses and stayed through the winter. It seems probable that the climate was milder at this time, for the grass remained green and they picked clusters of wild grapes; it was this that led them to name the new country Vinland the Good. When Leif reached home with stories of Vinland, his brother Thorvald decided to set out and see it for himself.

Relics of Viking armour (above) from Copenhagen, Oslo and London; a helmet of unusual design with "eye-pieces", a mail-shirt and a battle-axe. The Vikings' main weapons were the long-sword and the axe; one king, Eric of Norway, won the name "Blood-axe" through his prowess in battle with this weapon. Some of the Norse warriors, known as "bare-serks", would discard the mail-shirt and fight bare-chested in such blazing fury that we still speak of a madman "going berserk".

Thorfinn Karlsefni (far right). He failed to colonise the New World, five centuries before Columbus, as he might well have done, but the exploits of Thorfinn rank him as one of the greatest figures in the Viking epic.

An early American colony

Leif Eriksson came back to Greenland and settled down contentedly on his father's holding. However, his brother, Thorvald, set out eagerly for Vinland with a crew of thirty men. They found Leif's hut still standing, beached their ship and went exploring the islands and woods, while living on game, eggs, fish and the wild grapes. During their second summer, they moved up the coast and had gone ashore when, for the first time, they came across three natives who seem to have been a race akin to Eskimos rather than Red Indians. The Vikings immediately killed the strangers, but a fourth man escaped and it was not long before a war party arrived in canoes to avenge their murdered friends. On this occasion, the Skraelings, as the Greenlanders called them, were easily driven off, but Thorvald was killed by a chance arrow. So died the first white man in America. There are many theories about exactly where the Vikings landed and lived for several seasons; Vinland could have been Cape Cod, Martha's Vineyard or a score of places, but it is interesting to know that in 1963 a Norwegian expedition discovered nine buildings near L'Anse aux Meadows in northern Newfoundland and these dwellings date from about A.D. 1000. When the adventurers reached Greenland with news of Thorvald's death, another brother, Thorstein, set out to recover his body, but he met with bad luck and never found Vinland. The voyages were soon abandoned, and Vinland's very existence became a half-forgotten myth.

The settlers go home

One day in the summer of 1008, Thorfinn Karlsefni sailed from Iceland to Greenland. There he met Leif Eriksson, stayed with him at Brattahlid all winter and married his sister-in-law Gudrid.

Hearing the tales about Vinland inspired Thorfinn to fit out the largest expedition yet; three ships holding one hundred and sixty men, several women, provisions, cattle and poultry set sail in the spring of 1009, made landfall at Helluland ("slateland"), turned south to Leif's island and steered into a quiet bay which Thorfinn named Straumfjord.

One day Thorfinn's men saw the natives, the Skraelings, who watched them for a time from their canoes and then paddled away. Presently, they returned, bringing furs to barter for red cloth and the business was going along merrily until the Vikings' bull got loose and came out of the woods bellowing loudly. The Skraelings fled in terror and the Northmen prudently built a palisade to protect their little settlement.

This was a wise move because the natives turned hostile and there were pitched battles in which men on both sides were killed. By this time, a peaceful settlement was impossible and the settlers were beginning to quarrel over the women, so Thorfinn decided to abandon the settlement and return home.

Alfred Beats Back the Danes

The year 871 was a year of crisis. Wessex, the only English kingdom still able to resist the Viking invaders, was hard-pressed. The Vikings—or Danes, as they were now called—held most of Northumbria and all of East Anglia; they had overrun Mercia, ousted its king and put a puppet-ruler in his place. Now they were poised against Wessex and, from their base at Reading, they advanced into the heart of the kingdom. They met fierce resistance and, for once, a major defeat. But they came on again and Alfred, the young king, who had fought them again and again, was forced to ask for peace. He bought a five-year breathing-space in which to mend his broken kingdom, but it was not enough. By 876, when the truce was over, the Danes were stronger than ever. Guthrum, their leader, advanced by land, while a great fleet attacked along the south coast. Alfred fought stubbornly but, in January 878, disaster struck. Caught off guard while celebrating Twelfth Night, the Saxon fighting-men were scattered or slain, and with a handful of followers, Alfred fled into Somerset. It seemed as if there was no-one left to save England from falling into heathen anarchy.

A 19th-century artist's version of the legend that Alfred, while still a fugitive, entered the Danes' camp, disguised as a harper in order to learn the enemy's secrets.

King Alfred (870–899) shown on one of his silver pennies. At this time, there were several royal mints in the country.

"Be a king to my people. . . ."

Wessex had become the leading English kingdom after Egbert defeated the Mercians in 825. The Vikings were pressing in, but Wessex was well-organised to resist them. Alfred's father, King Ethelwulf, beat the Danes decisively but, as ever, the Danes came back. In 871, "fighting like a wild boar", young Alfred defeated them at Ashdown and, in the year when his brother Ethelbert died and he became king, he fought them in nine battles.

The disaster which caused him to flee into the marshes occurred at Chippenham where the Danes' surprise attack caught the Saxons off guard. But from his hiding-place, Alfred organised guerrilla warfare and eventually emerged at the head of an army which smashed the heathen host and penned the survivors in their fortified camp.

Instead of slaughtering the hated foe, Alfred acted with astounding mercy, sparing their lives and converting Guthrum to Christianity. He knew that he could not drive the Danes out of England, but he forced them to keep to their own territory—the Danelaw, while he re-organised his army and founded a fleet to tackle the enemy at sea.

He loved peace better than war and worked ceaselessly to repair his ravaged kingdom, encouraging the people to trade, to build and to obey the law; he brought monks and scholars from abroad, he founded schools and monasteries and himself learned Latin so that he could translate the Bible and other works.

Worn out by his labours, he died at fifty, murmuring, "Be a king to my people. . . ." He was the noblest man who ever occupied an English throne—the only one we have called "the Great".

Guthrum with his uncle, Harold Fairhair. After his defeat by Alfred, at Edington in 878, Guthrum accepted Christianity with the name of Athelstan. Later, he became ruler of East Anglia.

The Peace of Wedmore, 878

After the battle of Ethandune, Alfred had the enemy in the hollow of his hand. Shut up in their fortress near Chippenham, hungry, cold, many of them desperately wounded, the Danes could expect no mercy from the exultant Saxons.

Guthrum sent word that he would give hostages, if he and the rest of his men could depart unharmed. Alfred refused. Instead, he ordered Guthrum to come to his camp, with thirty of his battle-leaders. The Danes must have expected the worst as they passed through the ranks of the glowering Saxons to the King's tent. But Alfred made an astonishing proposition to his enemy; if they would quit his kingdom for ever and accept the Christian religion, he would not only spare their lives but he would share the land of England with them.

Overawed by such mercy, Guthrum agreed to be baptised with his leading men and Alfred himself, who stood godfather, called him his son and entertained him for twelve days before sending him back with costly gifts to his army.

England was divided by a line running roughly from the mouth of the Thames diagonally across country to the Mersey: the Danes were to live to the east and the north of this line in what was called the Danelaw, and an Englishman named Aethelred should rule western Mercia while Alfred, of course, retained Wessex. Guthrum, a man of honour, kept his word and departed to rule over East Anglia until his death in 890.

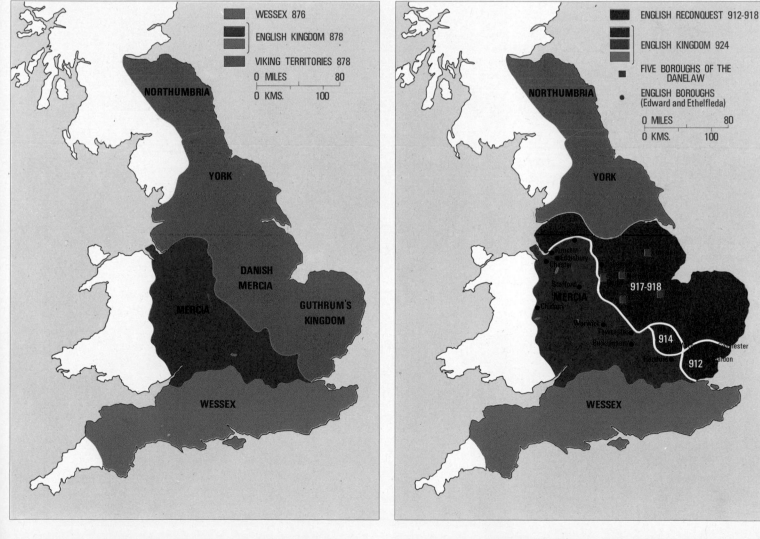

Here you can see the division of England as agreed by the Peace of Wedmore. The Danes kept eastern Mercia and East Anglia (Guthrum's kingdom), while further north lay the Danish kingdom of York (Northumbria) which had been one of the first areas to be seized by the Vikings. Alfred united Wessex and Mercia by marrying Ethelfleda, his daughter, to Mercia's ruler, Aethelred.

Alfred's pact was with Guthrum. Other Danish leaders were not bound to observe the peace, so Alfred occupied London and repaired its walls. After his death, his son Edward the Elder (900–926) and his daughter Ethelfleda, "the Lady of the Mercians", carried on the war and reconquered the Danelaw and its Five Boroughs. In 918 all the Danish leaders submitted to Edward as their lord.

The First Great King of England

How did the Danes manage to overrun kingdoms and seize whole districts of Saxon England? From the start they found that the country was extraordinarily ill-prepared for war: there was no fleet to guard the coasts, no town defences strong enough to repel a determined foe and no permanent army in the field, for the Saxons would serve for a time and then go home to tend their crops. In short, they had lost their old zest for war. Alfred tackled all these weaknesses. He planned a string of fortresses called "burhs" right across Wessex, for these would hold up an invader's progress; he rebuilt London's walls and ordered townsfolk to dig ditches and erect palisades round their townships. The army or "fyrd" was re-organised so that there were always troops at readiness as well as men on the farms and, most important, he built a fleet of warships which were bigger and faster than the Danish vessels. Finally, this great ruler showed himself to be a diplomat, for he made friends with the Welsh, came to terms with various Danish leaders and bound Wessex and Mercia together by the marriage of his daughter to the Earl Aethelred.

Alfred strengthens his defences
As a youth Alfred had noticed the Danes' skill in building strong camps which served as bases for attack and retreat. He therefore planned a network of "burhs" or boroughs to protect Wessex; the idea was to fortify existing towns and build new burhs so that no area would be without a place of refuge for the people. A thegn (noble) would organise the building of the ditched, stockaded strong-point and he would be bound to maintain a house there and to command the garrison. Alfred's son, Edward, used similar burhs to advance into the Danelaw.

Alfred had to put through his ship-building programme in the face of his people's lack of interest in sea-faring. He had the ships built to his own specifications and not as mere copies of Danish vessels. He had to employ Frisians who were professional sailors and navigators.

This mural from the Royal Exchange, London, shows Alfred directing the rebuilding of London's walls. His own capital was Winchester and the once glorious Roman city of London had long been in Mercian and therefore Danish hands. Despite the Peace of Wedmore, Alfred had to cope with outbreaks of Danish aggression, so, in 886, he captured London and decided to fortify it and hold it permanently. In this way, he would prevent the Danes from sailing up the Thames and penetrating the heart of the country.

Alfred the Law-Giver

Wessex had possessed a set of written laws long before most other kingdoms because, in 700, Ine, King of Wessex, had the best of the old laws and customs written down in a book called "The Dooms of Ine" ("doom" = law).

After the chaos caused by the Danish invasions, Alfred had to restore order in a kingdom where murder and robbery were everyday happenings. He therefore decided to re-write Ine's Laws, blending Christian teaching with old Germanic customs: at the beginning of his Book of Laws, he wrote, "That which you do not wish other men to do to you, do ye not to them. From this one doom, a man may decide how he may judge everyone rightly. He needs no other doom book."

Heard and interpreted in the Shire Courts and Hundred Courts (a "shire" was a county, a "hundred" a smaller district) the Laws of Alfred came to stand for justice and right.

Added to by his successors, they were the Laws of St Edward (the Confessor) which the Normans respected, and the foundation of Common Law in Britain and America.

An artist's view of Alfred giving judgement to a gathering of thegns and monks.

A Patron of Artists and Scholars

The St Matthew page in the Lindisfarne Gospels, an Irish-Saxon masterpiece produced in Northumbria. "Illuminating", as this art is called, began in Irish monasteries.

Artists and craftsmen

Before the Vikings ravaged the land and destroyed so many treasures of the churches and monasteries, English (especially Northumbrian) artists and craftsmen were known throughout Europe for their skills in illustrating manuscripts and in making altar vessels in silver and gold. Saxon masons developed great skill in carving stone ornaments and crosses. As in the manuscripts, Saxon artists were less clever in depicting human beings than in drawing and carving marvellously twisting animals and intertwined patterns of leaves, fruits and circles. Weapons, jewellery and church ornaments, too, were richly decorated and, despite the disasters of the invasion years, artistic skill did not entirely vanish. There were, however, fewer rich abbots and nobles to pay and encourage the artists.

However, Alfred devoted himself to rebuilding the smashed churches and monasteries, so that there came a revival of English art, especially painting and drawing. Another special skill of English craftsmen was the making of beautiful vestments and altar cloths which were superbly decorated with embroidery.

Though events forced Alfred to be a fighter for so much of his life, he was by nature a scholar—"from his cradle, he was filled with the love of wisdom above all things", wrote a friend, the Welsh monk Asser, whom like many others, he brought to Wessex to restore learning.

The King himself is said to have learned to read as a child, but there had been little time for other studies, so when the war was over, he mastered Latin with Asser's help and together they translated stories, religious works and Bede's great "History".

There is little doubt that Alfred inspired the beginning of "The Anglo-Saxon Chronicle". He was, indeed, a truly great man—a leader above all other leaders.

The Golden Age of Saxon England

Alfred died in 899 or 900. His son, Edward the Elder, was already a notable warrior, and when the Danes renewed their attacks, he struck back so hard that in a ten-year campaign the Danelaw (the Dane's own territory) was conquered. Thus Edward made himself undisputed king of all England south of the river Humber. His son, Athelstan, the third great warrior-king, carried on the work and after an overwhelming victory at Brunanburh, his dominions stretched from the Channel to the river Clyde in Scotland. As his coins proudly announced, he was "King of Britain". These three monarchs paved the way for the brilliant reign of Edgar (959–75) when Saxon England blossomed into a golden age of peace, art, learning and monastic reform. An English king, assisted by an English archbishop, ruled the whole country, a system of courts gave better justice than ever before, one coinage and one set of weights and measures were used everywhere and the English language came to be written as well as spoken. Yet, beneath this rule, a large Danish settlement covered the eastern side of the country, where the Danes followed their own customs and ways of life.

The tiny, 10th-century Saxon church at Bradford-on-Avon, Wiltshire. By this time, stone was beginning to be used instead of timber and we know that St Dunstan, for instance, when Abbot of Glastonbury, enlarged the church by adding a stone chapel. Not even cathedrals, however, were built on a vast scale, as in later years, when they were meant to impress men with their own littleness. Most Saxon churches were small and plain, though the masons cut their stone skilfully; notice the rounded door arch and scarcity of windows. The blank arches high up on the right are typical Saxon decoration.

A great reformer

Saint Dunstan, a great archbishop, was also an artist and musician; here you can see him writing with a quill pen which he sharpened with the penknife.

Dunstan, son of a thegn, was sent as a boy to the household of King Athelstan where his studious nature made him unpopular with the warlike young nobles. He therefore went to live with his kinsman, the Bishop of Winchester, and decided to become a monk.

Athelstan's successor, King Edmund, recalled him to Court and appointed him Abbot of Glastonbury and a royal counsellor. For several years, Dunstan practically ruled the kingdom but, during the brief reign of King Edwig, he fell from favour and was exiled to Flanders. Here he found that continental monks lived much stricter lives than any in England.

When Edgar became king, he recalled Dunstan and made him Archbishop of Canterbury. They improved the way in which the country was governed and reformed the monasteries by making the easy-going English monks obey the rules of the Benedictine Order. After Ethelred came to the throne in 979, Dunstan took no more part in the government but withdrew to Canterbury where he died in 998. He was made a saint soon afterwards.

Edgar the Peaceable

The reign of Edgar the Peaceable (who was said to have been rowed on the River Dee by six sub-kings) was a period of prosperity—a lull between the wars against the Danes and the fearful disasters to come. It was a time of church reform, when Dunstan and his bishops drove out the slack and lazy monks to replace them by monks who were pious and industrious. So, once again, English monasteries produced beautiful books, carvings and metalwork.

The country itself, including the Danelaw, was now divided into shires, each with its boroughs and sub-districts called *hundreds*. To each shire, Edgar appointed a shire-reeve or *sheriff* who saw to matters like taxation and justice in the various courts of shire, hundred or borough. Every man, though free, had to have a lord to whom he gave service and who was responsible for his good behaviour. And every man (at least in theory) had a say in everyday matters through the *moot* or meeting—the *hundred moot*, the *shire moot* and, greatest of all, the *Witan moot* when the lords or *ealdormen* met to advise the king. It was indeed the Golden Age of Saxon England.

Here is Edgar the Peaceable, at his coronation (at Bath, quite late in his reign), enthroned between St Dunstan, Archbishop of Canterbury and St Ethelwold, the energetic Bishop of Winchester—a great ouster of monks from the "decayed" monasteries.

A Single Kingdom

By the second half of the ninth century, the Vikings were seizing land and sharing it out like booty. They took part of Northumbria, East Anglia and most of Mercia. They tried to take Wessex, too, but Alfred drove them out. The peace he made with Guthrum was a treaty between equals. For they drew a line across England and the Saxons were to keep their side and the Danes to the Danelaw. This could not last. When Alfred's sons and grandsons conquered the Danelaw, the separate kingdoms vanished and, from about 940, there was, apart from short periods, only one king of England. The two peoples intermingled and intermarried, though the newcomers kept their language and laws and gave Scandinavian names to many places. They enjoyed town life and, because of their travels, knew more about trade than the English. Yet, in most ways, the English way of life was superior to the Vikings'; they converted them to Christianity and absorbed them into the population, so, apart from local customs, it soon became difficult to distinguish Saxon from Scandinavian. Though it still had to suffer invasion and defeat, the English nation had emerged.

This Saxon plough-team consists of the ploughman, four oxen and a boy to urge them on with a pointed goad. The sower was probably put there to complete the picture, because he would not normally sow right after ploughing. Notice the oxen are quite small and do not seem to be wearing yokes or collars; they are pulling a wheel-plough,

The Danish farmers

The Danes ploughed, sowed, reaped the same crops in the same way as the Saxons. Probably, the warriors lorded it over the local people, making serfs of some they had captured; the man who had won his land with his sword did not readily acknowledge a lord; he was not bound by customs of a manor and he saw no reason to hold his land as narrow strips in common fields. So, in East Anglia, there were many "freemen"— small farmers independent of a manor or lord; they might have certain duties to a superior but these sturdy fellows were not like the lowly villeins of the Midlands, who were counted among their lord's possessions as though they were his cattle.

Beekeeping was an essential occupation, for honey was the only sweetener and was much used to make a drink called mead. Cane sugar reached Western Europe from the East after the First Crusade; it arrived in the form of hard sugar "loaves".

A reconstructed Saxon house about the size of a small room. It was made with four corner-posts and posts in the middle of each end to carry the ridge pole. Walls were made of wickerwork (wattle) daubed with mud.

made of wood, apart from the iron coulter which cuts the soil ahead of the furrow-board. This illustration is probably a copy of an earlier original.

Ethelred the Unready

Edgar died in 975 and, almost immediately, the peace was shattered. The Danes came back, as fierce and as pitiless as ever. Places as far apart as Chester, Southampton and London were sacked with appalling ferocity, and the king, Ethelred, nicknamed "the Unready", was helpless. No warrior himself and unable to command the nobles, he tried to buy off the Danes with huge sums which had to be raised by means of a heavy tax called the Danegeld. Naturally, the Danes came back for more, so the people grew ever poorer without losing their terrible oppressors. For thirty years they suffered raids which grew to such a pitch of fury that, in 1013, they offered the crown to Sweyn, King of Denmark. Ethelred fled to Normandy and Sweyn died; his son Canute was opposed by Ethelred's valiant son, Edmund Ironside, who fought like another Alfred and had made a treaty dividing the island when he suddenly died; perhaps by poison. Thus England came to be ruled by Canute, as part of a Scandinavian empire that included Norway, Denmark, Greenland and the Scottish islands. But lands as scattered as these could not long be held together.

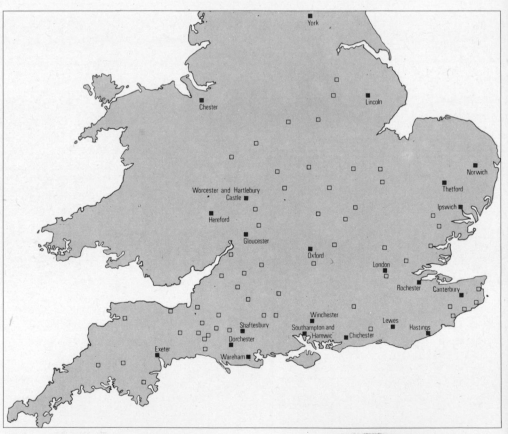

This iron spearhead was found in a grave at the great Viking base at Birka in Sweden.

Where the money for the Danegeld was minted: the map above shows the chief minting-places in Saxon England; on the right is a coin from the Lincoln mint. Athelstan declared, "there shall be one coinage in the king's dominions", and the standard of coin-making was remarkably uniform from so many mints. Coin types were changed every 6 years and, from 973, all mints had to use identical dies. The Danegeld was a terrible burden for the common people and even when the danger had passed, the tax was still imposed by Canute and William the Conqueror.

Sweyn Forkbeard

Sweyn Forkbeard, King of Denmark, first came to England to avenge the murder of his sister, Gunnhilda. Ethelred had given land to various Danish nobles on condition that they and their followers should fight for him against the raiders. When this foolish plan failed, Ethelred ordered every Dane living in England to be murdered. Among the slain were a noble named Pallig and his wife, Gunnhilda. Sweyn swore an oath of revenge and for several years came slaughtering and burning until, in 1013, the stricken people offered him the crown.

Left: When raiding, the Vikings would round up horses in the district. This improved their mobility and range. The Saxons fought on foot.

Sweyn, King of Denmark, sacked Winchester and Oxford in 1013. Though repulsed at London, he was proclaimed King, but died soon afterwards.

The king in Saxon England

Here you see the king, holding the sword of justice, sitting among his counsellors, the Witan. On the right is a gruesome reminder of the fate of a traitor.

In Anglo-Saxon England the early kings were no more than tribal chiefs, but the idea arose that Kings were descended from the gods, from Woden himself. Since, therefore, a king was to some extent a god, it was particularly wicked for an ordinary man to try to make himself a king.

A king did not necessarily have to be the eldest son, but he had to have royal blood in his veins. In times of war or when the dead king's son was a child, it was more sensible to choose, say, a grown-up brother of the king. Alfred, for example, was chosen instead of his brother's little son.

Who chose the king? This duty fell to the Witan, a body of counsellors who accompanied the king about his kingdom—they were "ealdormen" or powerful earls. If the king died suddenly, they had to act quickly, so they would choose his brother or son, according to his age, prowess or godliness. Solemn coronation, anointing with oil, crown, sceptre and gorgeous robes were all to emphasise the holy nature of kingship, and gave the king in Christian form the supernatural powers that the old pagan kings claimed through descent from the gods.

The Invaders Return

The return of the Danes brought disaster. Compared with the continent, Edgar's England was incredibly rich and peaceful, for the losses of Alfred's time had been made good and the Scandinavian settlers in the Danelaw had accepted Christianity and had taken to farming and trade. Then the storm broke. The Danes bled England white, plundering the churches and demanding vast sums in silver and gold—at least 15,000 English silver pennies have been found in Scandinavia and these would be only a tiny fraction of the loot taken back across the North Sea. Men like Olaf Tryggvason came simply to enrich themselves—he arrived off the Kent coast in 991 with 93 ships—three years later, he was back with Sweyn, plundering, slaying and collecting provisions and Danegeld. Some Scandinavians, like Thorkel the Tall and Pallig, Gunnhilda's husband, got paid for fighting for Ethelred, but the position was the same—English silver was taken by friend and foe. Sweyn Forkbeard and Canute came to rob and stayed as conquerors, yet Canute at least brought order, firm rule and, after his conversion, Christian principles to the troubled island.

"In battle with the heathen men"—a scene from a 12th-century *Life of St Edmund*, a king of East Anglia, who was killed by the Danes.

Remains of a cliff-top fortress on the Isle of Skye which was used as a look-out from which to give warning of the approach of Viking raiders.

Statue of Byrhtnoth of Essex outside All Saints' Church, Maldon. Olaf Tryggvason sailed up the Blackwater and demanded gold from the English drawn up on the river bank. Byrhtnoth stoutly refused. Chivalrously, but perhaps foolishly, he allowed the Vikings to cross unhindered, and was cut to pieces with his followers. This episode is commemorated in *The Battle of Maldon* one of the finest pieces of Anglo-Saxon poetry.

An Irish bronze crozier—the crook or staff carried by an abbot or bishop—found at Waterford Castle, Ireland. Perhaps it was hidden from the Vikings, for they regularly robbed the Irish churches and founded settlements at Waterford, Dublin, Limerick and Cork. Having stolen everything they could carry away, the Vikings took to honest trading.

A jewelled necklace with pendant cross found at Desborough, Northamptonshire. This would have been worn by a Saxon bishop or noble. The plunderers came looking for treasures of this kind which, like coins and altar vessels, could be easily carried off to the ships. They would give a monastery time to replenish its treasures before calling again!

The Dukes of Normandy

While the Vikings were plundering England, raiders also fell upon Northern France. From the ninth century, the country was constantly ravaged by the Northmen. They burnt Paris and occupied Rouen several times. Eventually Charles the Simple gave Rouen and the territory surrounding the city to Rollo, chief of the Northmen or Normans. Rollo, who accepted the French king as his overlord, was converted to Christianity. He died in 927 and, during the next century, the dukes of Normandy were engaged in enlarging their possessions. As you would expect, they proved to be warlike and, to guard their lands, they built towers which later developed into castles. But they were also excellent farmers, good builders in stone and they took to Christianity with zest. Many of their kinsmen fought in England and, not surprisingly, the Norman dukes took more than a passing interest in the fertile country across the Channel.

A medieval view of the grim, avaricious Normans. With their helmets, shields and lances, one can sense their disciplined ferocity.

The Early English Kings

The kings of Saxon England

The great kings of Alfred's house were his son, *Edward the Elder*, who reconquered the Danelaw and laid the foundations for *Athelstan* to become "King of all Britain". He defeated the Scots and the Vikings and ruled with justice and firm control. *Edmund* and *Edred* held on to his conquests but *Edwig* could not control the powerful earls. *Edgar* did not have to cope with Viking raids, and his reign blossomed into a glorious age. *Edmund Ironside* might have equalled the best of his ancestors, but he died young and it was left to *Canute* the Dane to prove once again that the kingdom could prosper only when it had a strong king. *Harold* had the qualities of a leader but was cursed with bad luck and an overdaring temperament.

Athelstan (925–40), advanced north of the Humber and added southern Scotland to his dominions. Faced by an alliance between the Scots and the Danes, he won a complete victory at Brunanburgh (937). Athelstan divided the Danelaw into shires, each having at its centre a market town which the Danes had established. He was the first Saxon King who could truly claim to be "King of Britain".

Edwig or Edwy (955–59), the young nephew of Edred, was a weak and irresponsible ruler. He drove St Dunstan into exile and provoked the earls of Mercia and Northumbria to rebellion in favour of his brother, Edgar, so that, by the end of his reign, he controlled only southern England. This defiance of the King by the great earls marks the weakness of the Saxon monarchy.

Edmund Ironside (1016) was made of much stouter material than his cowardly father. When Canute reappeared to carry on Sweyn's campaign, Edmund raised Wessex, defeated the Danes and, but for treachery, might have driven them into the sea. However, he and Canute had agreed to share the kingdom as in Alfred's day, when Edmund suddenly died, possibly from poison.

Alfred (871–900) is the only King of England to have been called "the Great". He saved Wessex and the Christian religion, defeated the Danes and made a treaty with them based on strength. Realising that he could not drive them out completely, he divided the kingdom but secured London. He revived learning and trade, rebuilt the devastated monasteries and gave his people order and justice.

Edward the Elder (900–25), son of Alfred, launched a counter-attack against the Danes. With the aid of his sister, Ethelfleda, he drove deep into the Danelaw, while she drew off their forces. As the allies advanced, they built *burhs* or fortified towns to hold their gains and these later became centres of trade. In this way, the Danelaw was conquered and did not remain a separate kingdom.

English Kings who were not of Alfred's line

Canute (1016–35), son of Sweyn Forkbeard, became King of England after Edmund Ironside. He ruled most of Denmark, Norway, Sweden and the Scottish Isles, and was the strongest monarch in Europe.

Hardicanute (1040–2), son of Canute, was the last of the Danish Kings of England. He seems to have been a worthless man and the English people gladly turned to the House of Wessex, and Edward.

Harold (1066) was chosen king by the Witan because he was a natural leader and a proven warrior. However his best troops were exhausted or absent when it came to fighting the Normans at Hastings.

Edmund (940–46), Athelstan's brother, was only eighteen when he dealt with an uprising of the Danes who tried to throw off his authority and set up a kingdom of York. He subdued them and conquered the ancient kingdom of Strathclyde. In return for an alliance, he granted Strathclyde to Malcolm of Scotland. Edmund had only reigned six years when he was murdered.

Edred (946–55), another brother of Athelstan, was chosen by a Witan that included Englishmen, Welshmen and Danes. This advance towards a united country was checked by Wulfstan, archbishop of York, who persuaded the Northumbrians to take Eric Bloodaxe as their king, but Edred drove him out. Edred, who suffered from ill-health, was greatly helped by his friend and adviser, St Dunstan.

Edgar the Peaceable (959–75) recovered the royal authority and, with St Dunstan's help, encouraged learning and the foundation of new monasteries. Not having to cope with Viking invasions, and strong enough to control the earls, he was able to devote himself to fostering peace and trade in the realm, so his reign came to be looked on as the Golden Age of Saxon England.

Edward the Martyr (975–8), Edgar's son by his first wife, was only thirteen when he became king and there immediately arose an opposition party which aimed to secure the crown for Ethelred, Edgar's son by his second wife. Whilst on a visit to his step-mother, Edward was murdered and, though everything pointed to the guilt of the Queen and her friends, Ethelred succeeded his brother.

Ethelred the Unready (978–1016), a cruel and foolish man, was totally unfitted to lead his countrymen against the Danes who fell upon the kingdom with murderous greed. His policy of trying to buy them off and his treachery towards his Danish subjects led to full-scale invasion by Sweyn Forkbeard. Ethelred fled to Normandy, but returned to London when Sweyn died.

Alfred the Atheling, one of the two sons of Ethelred and Emma of Normandy, came to England when Canute died, in hopes of recovering his father's throne. He fell into the hands of Godwin, a Saxon earl who had been high in Canute's favour, and was blinded at Ely, where he died of his injuries. This crime led to ill-will between the dukes of Normandy and the house of Godwin.

Edward the Confessor (1042–66), son of Ethelred, was brought up in Normandy, where he came to know the young duke William. His liking for Normans at Court led to a clash with Earl Godwin and to the banishment of the foreigners. Towards the end of the reign, the real ruler of England was Godwin's son, Harold, while the King devoted himself to religion and to the building the abbey at Westminster.

The Decline of Saxon England

Canute was a youth when he accompanied his father Sweyn Forkbeard to England. He saw Sweyn proclaimed King and when he died shortly afterwards, Canute returned home to take advice from his older brother. He soon returned with an army and was fought to a standstill by young Edmund Ironside, son of Ethelred, but a true descendant of Alfred the Great. They had agreed to share the kingdom when Edmund died and Canute therefore became king of several kingdoms—England, Denmark, Scotland and presently, Norway and part of Sweden. He liked England and ruled it well, but on his death his sons divided his possessions and within seven years the English throne was again vacant. In Normandy was living the son of Ethelred and Emma of Normandy; his name was Edward and he came to England and reigned there for twenty-four years. In later years he was called "the Confessor" but during his lifetime the kingdom was ruled mainly by Earl Godwin of Wessex, a powerful, unscrupulous noble whose son Harold became king in 1066. Edward left no son and the Witan chose Harold, so he was the rightful King even though he had no royal blood in his veins.

King, archbishop and warriors at sea in rough weather. Canute made many sea voyages in order to visit his dominions and to make expeditions against Norway and Sweden. He also journeyed to Rome in 1027 to see the Pope.

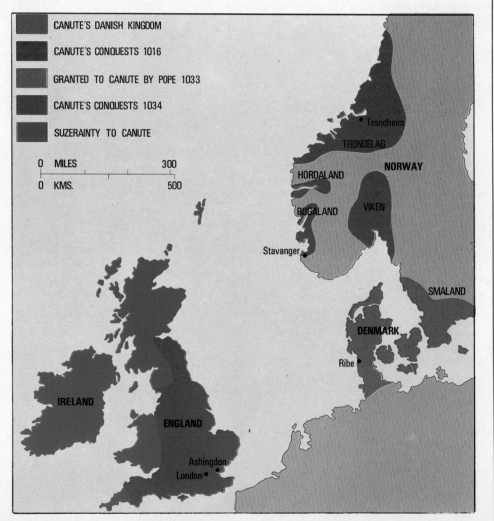

CANUTE'S DANISH KINGDOM

CANUTE'S CONQUESTS 1016

GRANTED TO CANUTE BY POPE 1033

CANUTE'S CONQUESTS 1034

SUZERAINTY TO CANUTE

0   MILES   300
0   KMS.   500

Trondheim
TRONDELAG
NORWAY
HORDALAND
ROGALAND
VIKEN
Stavanger
SMALAND
DENMARK
Ribe
IRELAND
ENGLAND
Ashingdon
London

The Kingdoms of Canute

The map shows Canute's sea-empire. After becoming King of England in 1016, he inherited Denmark and presently defeated both the Swedes and the Norwegians. Canute must have been a dynamic character to have ruled such widely separated lands; the English accepted his rule because he gave them order and justice.

Edward the Confessor

Brought up in Normandy, Edward absorbed the Normans' enthusiasm for Church affairs. Though more like a monk than a king, he was crafty enough to survive the bitter rivalry between his Norman friends and the English nobles and if, towards the end of his reign, he let Earl Godwin and Harold rule the kingdom, they were men of first-class ability. Called Saint Edward, he was England's patron saint for many years.

Scenes from the life of Edward the Confessor (above, left): we see the pious king comforting the sick and giving encouragement to a bishop at his prayers.
Edward the Confessor at Court (above, right). His greatest achievement in life was the building of Westminster Abbey.

Harold elected King

Edward died in January 1066. On his death-bed, he named Harold of Wessex as his successor, for the only direct descendant of Alfred was a boy, Edgar the Atheling (prince). The Witan, meeting immediately, chose Harold. Despite William of Normandy's claim that he had been promised the crown, the Witan did not even consider him. By right, Harold was King of England.

Here we see Harold, the rightful King of England, at his coronation. Soon after, his traitor brother Tostig joined forces with Harold Hardrada and invaded the north. Meanwhile, in Normandy, Duke William was assembling his own invasion force.

Harold Fights for his Throne

As soon as Edward had died and the Witan had named Harold as his successor, the kingdom, which had been weakened by quarrels between the great earls, was now in danger of attack both from the north and from across the Channel. In Canute's reign it had seemed as if England might have been drawn into the Scandinavian world; then, in Edward's time, it seemed as if his Norman friends had won the day, but Earl Godwin and his sons had restored the power of Wessex and the English. Now, with Edward dead and a commoner on the throne, the dangers re-appeared. Harold's traitor brother Tostig, exiled for his misdeeds, went to Norway where Harold Hardrada saw himself as a second Canute. Together, they planned an invasion of the north, a good starting point, because Harold would not readily find loyal support in that part of the country. Meanwhile, the Normans who, early in the Confessor's reign, had narrowly failed to gain a commanding position in the kingdom, were now preparing a landing somewhere along the south coast. Their grim Duke was known to have recruited a force of knights and landless adventurers.

Harold and William of Normandy

In 1064 Harold Godwinson was the greatest earl in England. He had proved himself a fine general, and King Edward, old and ailing, had long since left the kingdom in his care. Harold was much admired for his prowess and generosity, though the northern earls were jealous of his power.

One day, Harold was blown by a storm onto the French coast where the Count of Ponthieu held him for ransom until ordered to pass him on to his overlord, William of Normandy.

For months Harold remained half-guest, half-prisoner at William's court; the two men seemed to be the best of friends. But no ship was provided to take Harold home.

At last, William opened his heart; long ago, his kinsman, Edward the Confessor, had promised him England's crown and, with Harold's help, he was determined to get it. He would give Harold Wessex to rule if he would swear to support his claim.

The Englishman was trapped. He knew that the King had no right to give away the crown and, since he himself owned Wessex, he had no need to accept it as a bribe, but he saw that William would never release him until he promised. From England came news that the King was ill, so Harold swore the oath. With horror, he discovered he had sworn on the hidden bones of a saint. In the sight of men, the oath was now binding. However, Harold sailed for home and when he accepted the crown of England, he hardly considered the promise he had been tricked into making.

Above: After the battle: King Harold wee[...]

 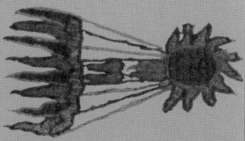

Two details from the Bayeux Tapestry: first, Harold is escorted to Duke William's court; second, the comet, omen of doom, appears in the sky. Astronomers confirm that it was Halley's Comet, seen about every 75 years.

Above: A parley before Stamford Bridge between Harold (left) and his brother, Tostig.

lain brother.   **Below: The Saxon army celebrating victory, but news arrives that the Normans have landed.**

William of Normandy

Duke William's claim to the throne of England was a highly dubious one. As a young man, early in the Confessor's reign, he had visited the English court and had apparently made a good impression on the King; both spoke French, of course; both were sincerely religious, and they were related to each other because the King's mother was great-aunt to William. He had, however, no blood-relationship with the English royal family. If Edward did promise that William should succeed him, he could only have done so subject to the Witan's approval, and nothing seems to have been known of such a promise in England. Clearly, William wanted to make aggression respectable, so he trumped up the story of a secret promise and, when Harold chanced to fall into his hands, tricked his most dangerous rival into swearing a solemn oath of support. This earned him the Pope's blessing and a sacred banner, but there can be little doubt that William had decided to make a gambler's bid for the English throne as soon as the childless Edward died. The whole operation was planned so that, if it failed, he could safely fall back to his own dukedom.

Head of a bishop's staff or crozier at the time of the Conquest. William greatly valued the support of the Church and he obtained the blessing of Pope Alexander II upon the invasion. Harold was regarded as an oath-breaker and his friend Stigand, Archbishop of Canterbury, had not been recognised as rightful archbishop.

Who was William of Normandy?

Robert the Devil, Duke of Normandy, fell in love with Arletta, a tanner's daughter of Falaise. Although he already had a wife, he took Arletta away to his castle and when he decided to go on a pilgrimage, he made the Norman barons swear to accept his son William as his heir. Robert died on his journey and a majority of the barons kept their word, though William was illegitimate and still a child.

For the next twelve years, the young duke was in constant peril; for a time, his relatives had to keep him in hiding. By this time, his mother had married a knight and William had two half-brothers, one of whom, Odo, later bishop of Bayeux, became his life-long friend. Not surprisingly, William grew up into a grim, relentless young man. From boyhood, he showed outstanding skill in battle and statecraft. He developed into a much harder character than his older cousin Edward, the exiled heir to the English throne who was living in Normandy since his father had been driven out by the Danes. Years later, he went to visit him in England where Edward may have promised him the crown. But, though he coveted England and conquered it, William remained a Norman at heart.

The first Norman king of England— William I seen on a medieval Roll of the Kings. Luck and military skill won him the throne.

Founder of the Normans' fortunes— Rollo the Viking, who obtained Normandy in 911 through a treaty with Charles the Simple, King of France.

The two lions of Normandy, Duke William's emblem, displayed on his banner as Harold displayed the dragon of Wessex.

Against all odds

William had to fight hard and pitilessly to master his dukedom. It had suited the barons well to accept a child as their lord, for they could defy his authority and ignore the dues which, as vassals, they should pay. They could pay off old scores and seize the lands of weaker men.

It was in this atmosphere that William grew up and learned to fight, to meet cunning with cunning and to match cruelty with merciless revenge. He was barely twenty when he narrowly escaped death at the hands of his cousin Guy who had plotted to overthrow him. William went for aid to his overlord the King of France, and crushed the rebellion.

It was not his last encounter with traitorous barons, but they came to know he was harder than any of them, a better soldier with a sharper brain, a master of castle attack and defence, and a man of enormous physical strength. Respect grew and, by the time he set out for England, he was already called the Conqueror, for he had beaten the Count of Anjou and had added Maine to Normandy. When he raised his invasion force, there was no shortage of volunteers for the English adventure.

The face of the Conqueror, glaring down from the façade of Wells Cathedral, Somerset.

Macbeth and the Kingdom of Scotland

In the eleventh century, Scotland was a wild country, lying beyond the fringes of civilised Europe. The north-eastern part had been inhabited by the savage Picts since before Roman times and, in the sixth century, the western part was settled by Scots who came from Ireland. During the period of Viking attacks, many Scandinavians occupied the northern and western parts of the mainland, so it is not surprising that this mixture of peoples had, as yet, no regular government. When Wessex grew powerful, Athelstan extended his rule to the Lowlands and two of the six "kings" who rowed Edgar on the Dee were Scots. Macbeth seems to have become King in 1040 by killing Duncan, probably in battle and not as in Shakespeare's play. Macbeth was succeeded in 1057 by Malcolm Canmore, a wily ruler who gave shelter to many Englishmen after the Norman Conquest. William the Conqueror invaded Scotland to force Malcolm to acknowledge him as overlord, but William Rufus had to go north to reassert this overlordship. Though Scottish kings were regarded as vassals of the English king, the Scots nevertheless managed to set up a separate monarchy.

Shakespeare's Macbeth, seen as a conscience-stricken murderer. He is ordering two ruffians to kill a noble named Banquo whom he feared. On the right are the three witches who prophesied Macbeth's rise and fall.

A gruesome picture (above) from *Holinshed's Chronicles of England, Scotland and Ireland* showing King Malcolm II watching an execution. This was a most bloodthirsty period in Scottish history.

Malcolm's ambition

At this time, Scottish succession went, not to the eldest son, but to a cousin or "tanist", and Malcolm II seems to have specialised in killing off tanists who might have dislodged him from the throne. This determined character won the sub-kingdom of Lothian from the Earl of Northumbria and defeated an army sent by Canute. Later, he probably had to submit to Canute, but managed to keep Lothian.

Holinshed's "Chronicles" appeared in Elizabeth I's reign, a curious collection of fact and legend, on which Shakespeare based the plots of "Macbeth", "King Lear" and his historical plays.

To murder for the crown

Here we see Macbeth being crowned and, below, a grim example of his royal justice, a multiple hanging.

How much *do* we know of Macbeth, Shakespeare's thane who killed his royal guest and was driven to commit further murders until he met his own violent death?

It seems that when Malcolm II secured the succession of his grandson, Duncan, a kinsman named Macbeth had a better claim. He and his wife Gruoch were both of royal descent and were not prepared to wait for the crown, since Duncan was not old, as in Shakespeare's play. The upshot was a royal feud and, in 1040, Macbeth slew Duncan and exiled his sons, Malcolm and Donald Bain.

Malcolm went to England, where Edward the Confessor supported him and eventually ordered an invasion of Scotland. Macbeth was defeated, but Malcolm carried on the war, pursued Macbeth to the north and killed him somewhere near Aberdeen in 1057.

Even then the men of Moray would not yield, but took Macbeth's stepson, Lulach, as their king. A year later, he too was dead and Malcolm III could feel secure. It was he who married the sister of Edgar Atheling and gave shelter to Englishmen after the Battle of Hastings; he had to submit to William I.

The Battle of Hastings

On the battle-plan below, you can see the two armies facing each other on Senlac Hill on 14th October 1066. Harold's army (left) stands on the hill-top, his force of house-carls in the centre and on either side (yellow), the men of the *fyrd* or national army, most of them hurriedly raised on Harold's march south. William's army consists of spearmen, archers and mounted knights, who have to advance uphill against the Saxon "shield-wall". They attack several times and are driven back. When the ill-trained fyrdmen see the Normans retreating, they break ranks and pursue them. The Normans turn and cut them to pieces—this is the position in the lower plan (left). William orders a massed charge, while his archers fire high into the air over the shield-wall. Harold is mortally wounded. At bottom right, nearly all the fyrdmen are scattered or dead and the remnants of Harold's bodyguard stand at bay as the Normans close in for the kill. The Saxons fight on until they drop beside their dying king. Even the Normans are awed by their courage but, in one day, the kingdom has been lost and won.

The Battle of Hastings

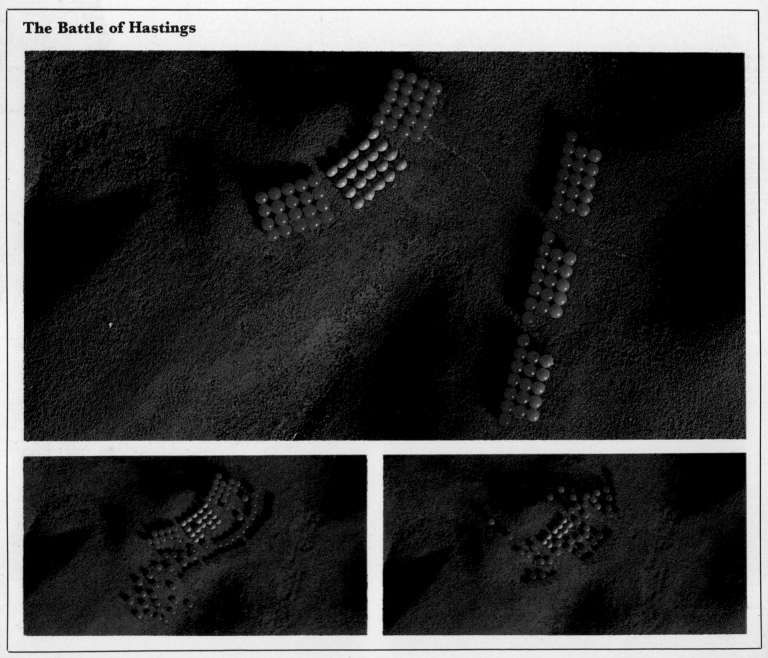

The battlefield today, from Harold's position on the hill; at that time it was a bare slope. The Saxons rode to battle but dismounted and fought massed close together on foot. William's use of heavily-armed cavalry had not been seen before in England and he had more and better archers. A more cautious man than Harold would have waited for the arrival of overwhelming reinforcements— which were marching towards Hastings.

The Bayeux Tapestry

This vivid masterpiece which tells us much about the Normans is not really a tapestry (in which the design would be woven into the material), but a superb piece of embroidery on a strip of linen about 80 yards long by 19 inches wide. It is worked partly in stem stitch and partly in laid work, with woollen threads in green, blue, yellow and grey. There is some doubt where the Bayeux Tapestry was made and for whom; one theory is that William's wife, Queen Matilda, ordered it, but it seems to have been made in Kent by Englishwomen under the direction of Bishop Odo of Bayeux. At all events, the Tapestry records the events leading up to the Norman Conquest; it starts with Edward the Confessor and goes on to show Harold during his enforced stay in Normandy and taking the oath; then comes the death of Edward, the crowning of Harold, the embarkation of William and his landing at Pevensey. Finally, we see the dramatic Battle of Hastings and the death of Harold. The original tapestry belongs to the town of Bayeux in Normandy, but there is a full-size replica in the Victoria and Albert Museum in London.

This scene from the early part of the Bayeux Tapestry shows an attack on the castle of Dinan in Brittany, when Harold was being "entertained" by Duke William who took him on an expedition against the Duke of Brittany. Harold thus gained an insight into the Normans' warlike skill—knowledge he might have used at Hastings. On the right, the keys of the castle are being held out on a lance as the garrison surrenders. This is one of the earliest pictures we have of a castle—a wooden tower on an earth mound, with a drawbridge over the ditch or moat. As you can see, the way to capture it was by direct assault, assisted by setting fire to the tower.

Here in miniature (below), is the main story of the battle. The Saxons, similarly armed to the Normans, stand fast, their shields locked together in a shield-wall. Their principal weapons are spears and two-handed axes. A Standard-bearer holds the flag of Wessex. The mailed Norman knights charge in close order, hurl their lances and then draw their swords. Against a static foe, they can attack at any point they choose.

Two soldiers of the *fyrd* run from the battlefield. Local levies, hastily collected by Harold on the march, they are armed only with clubs. If Harold had only waited, better-armed troops were on the road, marching to join his army.

One of the ships of William's fleet (above) about to set sail for England. William ordered ships to be built in ports along the French coast and, by August 1066, all were assembled at St Valery, at the mouth of the River Somme. For six weeks, contrary winds prevented the fleet from sailing, until the bones of a saint were brought from the church of St Valery. The effect was immediate. The wind changed, and William gave the order to hoist sail.

Here is a close-up (right) of two of the Normans who fought at Hastings. You can see the skill of the needle-women who have managed to depict chain-mail and the exact shape of the helmets.

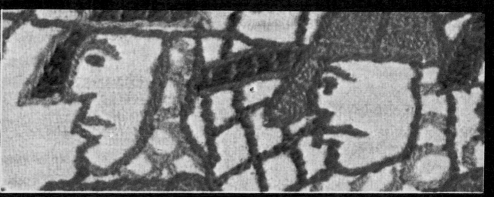

The Norman Estates

William took pains to make it clear that he had come as rightful heir of Edward the Confessor, and had merely overthrown a wicked usurper. However, having won a kingdom, he made sure that he would keep it in his iron grip. He rewarded his followers with estates and manors, but these were not outright gifts; in return, the barons had to provide knights for the royal army.

The King reserved vast estates for himself and the Church; his authority was immense and he meant to have none of the troubles he had known in Normandy. Castles were quickly erected to overawe the native population and every baron and knight in the land had to acknowledge William as his lord; the whole country was his and his alone to give or take away from his subjects. Along the borders of Wales, he gave grants of lands to earls who were to defend his frontier against Welsh tribesmen, and he entered Scotland in order to force Malcolm Canmore to accept him as overlord. But he made no attempt to conquer either country—the land of England was enough for William.

Saxons (above) are forced to dig a ditch and pile up earth for a castle mound. William's castles were *motte-and-bailey* type—wooden towers on earth mounds. He erected at least 100 of these strongholds at strategic points in the kingdom, where they dominated towns and possible centres of rebellion. He started only one stone castle—the Tower of London—and that was not finished in his reign.

The map (right) shows how William broke up the great earldoms of Saxon England and scattered them across the kingdom. This was an essential ploy in his policy of not allowing a subject to become too powerful in one part of the country. Notice how widely scattered were the 790 manors he granted to Robert Mortain. Only in exceptional circumstances did he allow a baron to build his own castle.

Carlisle

Newcastle on Tyne

Durham

Robert of Mortain

Alan of Brittany

Hugh d'Avranches

Robert of Mortain

William of Percy

Archbishop of York

York

Gilbert de Gand

Bishop of Durham

Roger of Poitou

William of Warenne

Gilbert de Gand

Roger of Poitou

Roger de Busli

Alan of Brittany

William Peverel

William of Percy

Chester

Hugh d'Avranches

Roger de Busli

Lincoln

Henry de Ferrers

William Peverel

Ivo Taillebois

Derby

Alan of Brittany

Nottingham

Shrewsbury

Henry de Ferrers

Ivo Taillebois

Stafford

William of Warenne

Norwich

Roger de Montgomery

Leicester

Thorkill of Arden Count of Meulan

Roger Bigod

Warwick

Countess Judith

William Peverel

Huntingdon

Ely

Thorkill of Arden Count of Meulan

Northampton

Cambridge

Roger Bigod

Hereford

Worcester

Countess Judith

Alan of Brittany

Richard of Clare

Aubrey de Vere

Gloucester

Colchester

Aubrey de Vere

Oxford

Henry de Ferrers

Wallingford

London

Rochester

Bristol

Windsor

Odo, Bishop of Bayeux

Canterbury

Geoffrey, Bishop of Coutances

Richard of Clare

Dover

Winchester

Bishop of Winchester

Old Sarum

Richard of Clare

Robert of Mortain

Bramber

Robert of Mortain

Exeter

Robert of Mortain

Roger de Montgomery

Lewes

Pevensey

Hastings

Corfe

Arundel

William of Warenne

Robert of Mortain

NORTHUMBRIA (Siward)

(Beorn)

PRINCIPALITY OF GRUFFYDD AP LLYWELYN

MERCIA

(Leofric)

EAST ANGLIA (Harold)

(Ralph)

MORGANNWG

(Sweyn)

WESSEX (Godwin)

COUNTY BOUNDARIES

CASTLES BUILT BY WILLIAM 1 OR WITH HIS SANCTION

0 MILES 60

0 KMS. 80

79

William as Ruler

William did not introduce the feudal system into England. To some extent, it already existed, but in place of the Saxon idea that every man should have a lord and that a freeman might change his lord if he liked, William tied men much more closely to the land and to one lord. He himself stood at the apex of a pyramid; beneath him were the greater tenants-in-chief (earls, barons, abbots, bishops), below them came lesser tenants (knights, country towns) and below them again came the people who lived and worked on the land (freemen, villeins, serfs). With every acre of land went some form of service—military service, rents, gifts and duties. William took good care to build up his own riches—over 1000 of the best manors were his own, he taxed the people mercilessly and went on collecting Danegeld. He allowed no baron to become over-powerful, and the castles which he built so speedily were garrisoned by his own men under his own constables. He was, in fact, an absolute ruler—dynamic, determined and ruthlessly cruel, yet, even in the eyes of the English, he was a better man and more just than any of his barons.

The new order. Alan of Brittany swears allegiance to William for the lands of Edwin, the former Saxon Earl of Mercia. At first William confiscated only the lands of those who had fought against him, but later he seized all the major estates of the Saxon nobility.

How William ruled

The Norman Conquest transformed England. A new aristocracy of about 200 Norman lords shared the land; Norman sheriffs controlled the shires, Norman bishops took the place of English clergy and a council of Norman barons (the *Curia Regis*) replaced the old Witan. French and Latin took over as the languages of the ruling class, French churches and monasteries went up all over the country and French manners were adopted at Court. The kingdom was organised to produce a powerful royal army, and even the abbots and bishops had to equip numbers of knights in return for Church lands.

Yet, in some ways, William kept English laws and customs and, indeed, he and his successors were constantly quoting the laws of Edward. The shire organisation and local courts remained as they were, for William saw that the office of *sheriff* would suit him well. His sheriffs collected royal dues, presided over the shire-courts and made certain that everyone fulfilled his duty towards the king.

On the Continent, lesser tenants (e.g. knights) often supported their immediate lord against all comers, including the king himself, and to guard against this happening, William summoned every landholder, great and small, to meet him at Salisbury and to swear to support him above all other men. This was the "Oath of Salisbury", 1086.

A monk who had observed William closely at Court, wrote this about him in the "Anglo-Saxon Chronicle": "He was a very wise and great man . . . but severe beyond measure to those who withstood his will. He wore his crown three times every year . . . at Easter he wore it at Winchester, at Pentecost at Westminster, and at Christmas at Gloucester. And at these times all the chief men of England were with him, archbishops, bishops, abbots, earls, thegns and knights. So also he was a very stern and wrathful man. . . . He removed bishops from their sees, and abbots from their offices and at length he spared not his own brother, Odo."

"Amongst other things, the good order that he established must not be forgotten; it was such that any man might travel over the kingdom, with a bosom full of gold, unmolested; nor durst any man kill another, no matter how great the injury he had received from him."

"Being sharp-sighted in his own interest, he surveyed the kingdom so thoroughly that there was not a single hide of land of which he knew not the possessor and how much it was worth. . . . He enacted laws that whoever killed a hart or a hind should be blinded . . . and he loved the tall stags as if he were their father."

William defies the Pope

The Pope had blessed William's expedition and, in return, William intended to support the Church and to enrich it with grants of land. He was a religious man and his first step was to send for his friend Lanfranc, the Italian-born Abbot of Caen, and presently to make him Archbishop of Canterbury.

Lanfranc believed that the clergy should be organised and disciplined, that they should not marry, enjoy worldly pleasures, nor make money by taking several positions or offices. Lanfranc and the King reformed some of the slack Saxon monasteries, built

Lanfranc was a teacher before becoming archbishop.

new ones, appointed Norman abbots, and founded some schools. Magnificent new churches began to arise all over the country, in many of which English and Norman masons worked together, using fine Caen stone brought across from Normandy.

But while William supported Lanfranc and allowed the Church to have its own courts, he intended to be head of the English Church. He politely refused to do homage to the Pope for his new kingdom and would not allow him to appoint bishops. No-one, not even the Pope, could interfere with William's royal power.

An 11th-century picture of the Normans—tough fighters, military engineers, builders, lawyers, administrators. Quite a small group of Normans went to southern Italy and carved themselves a kingdom there.

Hereward the Wake

The legendary story opens when Hereward, accused by a priest of robbing a church, leaves home after a quarrel with his saintly mother, Lady Godiva.

Before setting out, Hereward bids farewell to his uncle, Abbot Brand.

He is proclaimed an outlaw and rides away to a life of adventure with his faithful servant, Martin Lightfoot.

He joins a Viking crew and sails overseas in search of fame and fortune, but

Hereward and Torfrida of Provence,

After many adventures, Hereward returns to his home, Bourne Manor, in Lincolnshire, where he slaughters the Normans occupying his hall.

Disguised as a potter, Hereward sees William of Normandy for the first time.

In revolt, Hereward leads a Viking army and captures Peterborough. Here, he saves a girl from warriors.

His stronghold, Ely, is lost; Hereward decides to kill his beloved mare, Swallow.

The rebellion has failed, but Hereward is pardoned by William. He goes to Winchester to swear allegiance.

Serving William abroad, Hereward is betrayed by jealous Norman knights and is killed in battle.

The Domesday Book

Although one could say that William won his kingdom in a single day by a single battle, he had many problems to solve before he could feel that his prize was secure. Normandy itself was a tremendous source of trouble, and he was there on a visit when the first English revolt broke out. William returned and put down risings in the West Country, in Mercia and Northumbria. At first, he acted mildly but when, with Danish help, a second uprising occurred, he marched north and took a most savage revenge upon the countryside. Hereward the Wake's stronghold at Ely was captured, Saxon lords were stripped of their land and, for the last fifteen years of his reign, William was absolute master of the kingdom. There were no more uprisings. Like many another successful man, William wanted to know how much he was worth and this was not pure greed, but a love of order and efficiency—if he knew exactly the size and value of every farm in the country, he would know exactly how much tax the people should pay. So, in 1086, he sent his officials round England to compile an astonishingly detailed tax return. It was called the Domesday Book.

Killing a pig: peasants could rarely afford to eat any meat except bacon.

Harsh Norman laws

William made few changes in the Saxon system of laws but, by ruthless punishment, he made sure they were kept—the penalty for killing a deer was to be blinded, for robbery the penalty was death or the loss of a hand, for the murder of a Norman, severe punishment was laid on the hundred in which the crime took place.

He enforced the old system of *tithings*, groups of ten men all responsible for the others' good behaviour and the chief *tithingman* had to report and pay for wrongdoing.

Trials by Ordeal—fire and water —were still used and a new one was introduced—Ordeal by Combat, in which the accuser fought the accused, armed with shields and special maces, and the loser was put to death.

What did the Domesday Book record?

The Domesday Book—the name means that the evidence in it was so exact that it would last until Domesday (the Day of Judgement)—consists of two volumes, written on sheepskin by William I's clerks in the last year of his reign. It can still be seen at the Public Record Office in London.

It was compiled like this: in each main area a panel of royal justices summoned a jury (twelve good men sworn to tell the truth) from each hundred (district) to check the word of barons and lords. All had to answer twelve questions; the first three were: What is the manor called? Who held it in the days of Edward the Confessor? Who holds it now? The remaining questions went into detail: how much ploughland, woodland, pasture? How many ploughs, oxen, sheep? What crops did the land produce? How was it shared among the villagers?

The information was written down. It recorded in detail the whole wealth of England. Then the books were sent to the Treasury at Winchester, where a "digest" was made of the information. This should have produced a single Domesday Book

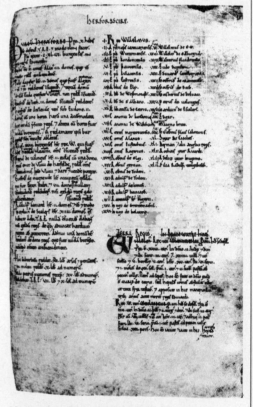
How the Domesday Book was written: a page from the Hertfordshire survey.

but, perhaps because of William's sudden death, there are two volumes. The first contains the "potted" versions of the large areas and the second is the survey of East Anglia which is not abbreviated and therefore is even more valuable to historians.

The King's Men

The terms baron, lord, earl and so on need some explaining because their meaning has gradually changed. A baron was simply a tenant-in-chief of the king, to whom he owed military service; he would fight in the royal army and bring with him so many knights according to the amount of land he held. In time, "the barons" came to mean the powerful nobles who attended the Great Council.

"Baron" was not a title like "earl", which William gave only to the greatest landowners. "Count" was rarely used but an earl's lady was the "countess" and his estates might comprise a "county". By the end of the Conqueror's reign all the earls were Normans, but there were still numbers of English "thegns", a term which died out in favour of "franklin" and "knight of the shire".

A lord was anyone who held a manor—one manor or a score—and therefore acted as "lord of the manor" in the Manor Court; but "lord" did not become a title of honour until the fourteenth century. The lord's tenants had duties to him just as he had duties to the king—he held his estates on condition that:

(i) he gave military service,
(ii) he attended the king's court,
(iii) he paid certain taxes or "reliefs" e.g. when he inherited his father's land,
(iv) he accepted the king's right to hold an estate when the heir was a child or to arrange for the marriage of an heiress. When the King increased their dues, the barons rebelled.

An illuminated capital letter: a knight paying homage to the King.

Villeins had to plough the lord's land before attending to their own. Oxen were used, never horses.

The poor peasant

The position of the workers—peasants on the manor—became worse under Norman rule. In Saxon times, there were slaves (thralls) but there were also many freemen who were tied lightly, if at all, to an overlord. Under the Normans, all land belonged ultimately to the king and, since everyone held it of him or of some tenant, no man could be free. Slavery died out, but the peasants came to have less and less freedom. A man was tied to the land. He could not leave and go to live somewhere else; he and his family belonged to the manor and if it was sold, they were sold with it as part of its wealth. He was subject to his lord's justice and to the rule of his officials.

Yet peasants looked to their lord for protection and they had certain rights—in the common fields, in the woods and to holidays—which the lord's steward usually respected. Generally speaking, the people of the manor were *villeins*, who held strips in the common fields, did "week work" two or three days a week for the lord and made certain payments, such as a lamb at Easter, tenpence at Michaelmas and a fee when a daughter married or when a son went to school.

There were a few *freemen* who paid rent for their land instead of doing week-work and there were *bordars* and *cottars* who held only the gardens round their cottages and did work on the manor for wages. The lowly condition of the peasants was emphasised by the fact that the ruling class spoke a different language, Norman-French.

Robert Curthose (Shortlegs), William I's rebellious son, a great fighting-man but too easy-going to win the respect of his barons.

Time Chart: the main events in world history

British Isles and Ireland

Lying on the western edge of Europe and, since about 5000 B.C., cut off from the mainland by a sea channel, Britain received invaders, metals, tools, civilisation and Christianity later than the rest of the continent. This separation brought some advantages and many disadvantages.

Europe

From Italy, conquest, trade, town-planning and organised living spread to the north and west. After Rome's fall a number of kingdoms emerged.

Date	British Isles and Ireland	Europe
c. 100,000 B.C.	Old Stone Age—few nomadic inhabitants in Britain.	Hunters using hand-axes and fire.
c. 10,000	Middle Stone Age—hunting, cave- and hut-dwelling.	Use of spears, bows, boats, crude pottery.
c. 6000	New Stone Age—polished flint-tools, flint-mining, pit-dwellings, corn-growing.	Fortified settlements, farming.
c. 3500	Barrow burials.	Minoan civilisation, Crete: cities, sea-trade,
c. 2500		fine pottery, parchment.
c. 2000	Bronze Age—but metal not widespread in Britain.	Mycenaean civilisation in Greece.
c. 1800	Stonehenge began to be built.	
c. 1500	Beginning of trade in gold, tin, amber.	
c. 1200	First arrivals of Celtic people.	Trojan War. Phoenicians trading.
c. 1000		Iron tools and weapons beginning to be used.
c. 750	Celtic settlements, villages, arable fields.	Rome founded. Rise of Greek cities.
c. 500	Tribal warfare, hill-forts.	Greeks defeated Persians. Athens supreme.
c. 330	Northern and western tribes still hunters and pastoralists	Alexander the Great ruled Greece.
c. 250	while southern Britain had contacts with continent and trade	Rome defeated Carthage and began to dominate
c. 200	in Mediterranean goods.	Mediterranean lands.
c. 100	Belgic tribes settle in south-east.	Riots in Rome but empire expanded.
54	Caesar's first expedition.	Gaul conquered.
0	Romanisation of south-east.	Roman civilisation at its peak.
A.D. 100	Claudius invaded Britain. London founded. Boadicea's rebellion crushed. Agricola conquered Wales and much of northern Britain. Roads, towns, fortified camps built to turn south and midlands into a Roman province.	Provinces in Europe mostly peaceful and prosperous, but in Rome, government by Emperors became increasingly violent and corrupt. Nero rebuilt city after the Fire.
	Hadrian's Wall built to defend and mark northern limit of the Empire.	Galen wrote medical books. Rule of the "Five Good Emperors".
200	Christianity began to make converts.	Spread of Christianity.
	Emperor Severus in Britain to restore order after attacks by northern tribes.	Diocletian divided the Empire into two parts. He persecuted Christians.
300	Carausius, admiral of Roman fleet, made himself Emperor of Britain.	Goths, Vandals and other barbarians began to attack the frontiers.
	Saxons increased their raids on east coast. Magnus Maximus set up as Emperor. Wall overrun and widespread attacks by Picts, Scots and Saxons.	Emperor Constantine founded Constantinople and made it the capital. Empire under severe pressure from barbarians.
400	Stilicho restored order temporarily.	
	Roman troops left Britain; attacks of Picts, Angles and Saxons increased. Jutes settled in Kent. St Patrick converted Ireland.	Rome sacked by Alaric's Visigoths and, later, by the Vandals. Barbarians overran Western Empire and settled in former provinces. Gothic kingdom set up in Italy.
500	Britons, possibly led by Arthur, gained victories over the invaders.	
	Anglo-Saxon settlement of eastern side of Britain. St Columba went from Ireland to found Iona.	The Franks settled in western Europe. Lombards dominated N. Italy. Benedictine Order founded.
600	St Augustine arrived in Kent.	Rise of the Pope's authority.
	Conversion of Northumbria by St Aidan. Synod of Whitby.	Emperor Heraclius at Constantinople restored some of Rome's prestige. Byzantine fleet powerful in Mediterranean.
700	Irish monasteries sent scholar-missionaries to many parts of Europe.	Constantinople besieged by Moslems.
	Venerable Bede writing at Jarrow. Offa of Mercia supreme in Britain.	Arab conquerors occupied Spain. Charlemagne, King of Franks, made wide conquests and spread Christianity: became Holy Roman Emperor.
800	First attacks of the Northmen occurred towards end of century.	
	Norse attacks increased; Danes settled in Ireland and Norwegians in Scotland. Egbert became King of the English; Danish conquest of England halted by Alfred the Great—Peace of Wedmore. England divided. London rebuilt.	Vikings attacked W. Europe, penetrated Mediterranean and Russia. Settled in Normandy. Learning flourished in Italy.
900	Anglo-Saxon Chronicle begun.	
	Edward the Elder and Athelstan defeated Danes and extended English rule to Scotland. The government of Edgar and Dunstan produced Golden Age of Saxon England.	Christianity spread to Scandinavia and E. Europe. Byzantine Empire strong but Danes all-powerful in the west.
1000	Ethelred the Unready—return of the Danes.	
	Massacre of Danes led to savage raids, conquest of the country and Canute's reign. English line restored with Edward the Confessor. Macbeth killed Duncan of Scotland. Norman Conquest of England and invasion of Scotland.	Norman kingdom in S. Italy; the Emperor submitted to the Pope. Urban II preached the First Crusade, and Crusaders set out from W. Europe.
1100	Domesday Book. Civil War in Ireland.	

Asia

From similar Stone Age beginnings, a dozen civilisations arose in Asia. The arts and sciences flowered more generously than in Europe.

River valley settlements in India and China. Farming began.
Town life in Sumeria, temples, trade.
Indus civilisation, cities, baths, furniture, temples, pottery, wheel.
Hsia Dynasty, China; plough, astronomy, maps, silk manufacture.
Hittites using iron. Aryans invaded India.
Shang Dynasty—earliest Chinese writing.
David, King of Israel.
Warlike Assyrian Empire.
Feudal system in China. Buddhism, India.
Alexandria reached India and founded an empire.
Mauryan Empire, India—Asoko.
Han Dynasty, China (400 yrs) Silk trade, astronomy advanced, musical notation invented.

Birth of Christ.

Since Asoko's death, India divided into warring kingdoms.
Emperor Ming-Ti introduced Buddhism into China—art, literature and science flourished.

Sanskrit, a literary language, in use in India.
Han Dynasty in China—a period of peace, prosperity and artistic achievement. Paper invented.

Han Dynasty ended and China invaded by nomad tribes from the north.

Gupta Empire in N. India was Golden Age of Hindu civilisation. Sanskrit literature, music, science and mathematics were studied. Temple architecture, sculpture, paintings of great beauty.

Japanese adopted Chinese language.
Towards end of century, Gupta Empire suffered attacks by Huns and Turks from central Asia.

Scholars from Athens migrated to Persia.
The Eastern Emperor ruled the remnants of the Roman Empire from Constantinople.
Japanese clan system led to Emperorship.

Birth of Mohammed and rise of Moslem faith.
Sui Dynasty re-united China, then T'ang gave it an enduring system of government that lasted until 20th century.

T'ang period of great artists—Chinese paper-making spread through Moslem world.

Moslems penetrated India—endless wars.

Persian literature and poetry.
Chinese were producing newspapers.

Period of fine Chinese painting but civil strife in China and Japan. Revival of Deccan art in India. Chinese invented gunpowder and produced an encyclopaedia.

Omar Khayyam writing Persian poetry.
Seljuk Turks moved into Middle East—attacked Constantinople, captured Jerusalem.
Printed books in China.

Africa

Apart from Egypt, we know so little about Africa Man probably first walked in East Africa. He built great walls in Rhodesia. What else?

Man using stone tools in E. Africa.

Corn-growing in Egypt; brick houses, Pyramids, ships, papyrus.
Middle Kingdom, brilliant period with vast temples, cities, trade, writing, superb craftsmanship. Cult of the dead.

Moses led Hebrews out of Egypt.

Assyrians conquered Egypt (671).
Persian conquest of Egypt.
Alexandria, centre of science, medicine.
Ptolemies ruled Egypt.

Egypt a Roman province.

Egypt and North Africa ruled by Rome—sophisticated town life and advanced agriculture.

Ptolemy writing about astronomy and geography.

First algebra book written at Alexandria.

Iron Age in Rhodesia.
Christianity established in Abyssinia.

Civil war and religious troubles in Egypt. The country, nominally ruled by the Emperor at Constantinople, fell into weakness and disorder for the next 200 years.

Egypt conquered by Moslem invaders—whole of N. Africa fell into Arab hands.

Acropolis at Zimbabwe, Rhodesia.

Egypt invaded by Fatimids—Cairo became capital.
Giant walls built at Zimbabwe.
Empire of (ancient) Ghana exported gold.

Trade flourished between Egypt and Italy.
Ghana defeated by Almoravids of Mali, Sudanese people who were converted to Islam.

The Americas

Early man came to America from Asia and took to hunting and farming. He raised temples but never really progressed beyond the Stone Age.

Man crossed Behring Strait into N.A.
Mammoth, bison-hunters.
Settlers in Peru.

Lakeside farmers in Mexico.
Pottery-makers at Tlatilco.
Sculptures and hieroglyphic writing of Olmec civilisation in Mexico.

Brilliant textiles of Paracas culture, Peru.

Beginning of Classic Maya period (c. 300 to 900).
Monte Alban temples built in Oaxaca, Mexico.

Mayan temple-cities; astronomy studied and accurate calendar compiled.

Mississippi Valley culture.

Huge pyramids built at Teotihuacan.

Mayan temple-building in Chiapas and Copan. Wall-paintings.

City of Machu Pichu in Peru.
End of classic Maya period.
Norwegians founded a colony in Iceland.

Marvellous city of Tula built by the Toltecs of Mexico.
Viking colonies set up in Greenland.

Leif Eriksson discovered Nova Scotia.
Norwegians stayed in Vinland.

Chimu people created a coastal empire in Peru.

Index

Lindisfarne Gospel: 37, 55
London: 11, 14, 26, *28*, 54, 60*f*, 65

Macbeth: 72*f*
Maldon, Battle of: *63*
marsh village: *see* village
Martha's Vineyard: 50
Mercia: *see* Saxon Kingdoms
mineral wealth: 6
monasteries: 36*f*, 40, 42*ff*, 52, 55*ff*, 80*f*
money: 5, 60, *see also* coinage and taxation

Neolithic Period: *see* Stone Age
Nero: 11, 15
Newfoundland: 50*f*
New Stone Age: *see* Stone Age
Norman Conquest and settlement: 3, 73*f*, *75*, 76, 77, 80, 83*ff*; warfare: *44*, 63, *74–77*
Normans: 48, 63, 68, 70, 76, *81*
Norsemen: *see* Vikings
North America: *see* Vikings
Northumbria: *see* Saxon Kingdoms
Nova Scotia: 50

Picts: 16, 22*f*, 25, 27, *28*, 36, 72

roads: 19
Rollo: 48, 63, 70
Roman architecture and town planning: *11*, *17*, 18*f*; army: 9, 13, 15; arts: 18; defences: *22*, *28f*; education: 19; Empire: 8, 15*f*, 22–25; invasions and occupation: 3*f*, 6, 9*f*, *11f*, 14, 18, 22, 25*ff*, 29; recreations: 19*f*; religion: *17f*, *20f*; ships: 9, *22*; trade: 18*f*; weapons: 8, *10f*, 13

Saint Aidan: 36, 40
Saint Augustine: 41
Saint Columba: 36, 40
Saint Cuthbert: 36, 41, 44
Saint Dunstan: 56, 57
Saint Patrick: *28*, 36*f*, 40
Saxon agriculture and food: *29*, 39; arts and architecture: *25f*, 38, *39*, 42, 55, *56*, 57, 62; defences: 29, 32, 52, 54, 61; invasions: 3, 22, 25–28, 34; kings and kingdoms: 26, 34*f*, 38, 44, 53*f*, 61, 64*ff*, 68, 78, 84; recreations: *29*; religion: *25f*, *28*, 38; settlement: 26, 29; weapons: *26*, 28, *29*, *39*, 55, 74, *75ff*; *see also* Sutton Hoo treasure
Scotland: 5, *7*, 16, 22, 25, 27, 42, 46, 56, 60, *62*, 64, 66, 72*f*, 78
ships: Roman: 9, *22*; Saxon: *26f*, *38*, 54; Viking: 44, *45*, 48, *50*; Norman: *77*
shire: 55, 57, 80
social structure, *see* community

Stilicho: 23*f*, 27
Stone Age: 2, *4*, 5, 7
Stonehenge: 6
Sutton Hoo treasure: 38, *39*
Sweyn, King: 60*ff*, 66
Synod of Whitby: 40, *41*

taxation: 19, 57, 80*ff*
Thames, River: 4, 9, 26, 53*f*
Thorvald: 50*f*
tools: *see under* appropriate period
trade: 28
transport: 19

U.S. law, foundation of: 55

Viking invasions and settlement: 3, 42, 44*f*, 48*f*, 52, 58, 61, *62*, 63*f*, 70, 72, 83; in North America: 46, 50*f*; religion: 48*f*; ships: *see* ships; warfare: *44*, 45, *46*, 60
village: 5
Vinland: 46, 50*f*
Vortigern: 23

Wales: *4*, 10, 18, *34*, 36, 40*f*, 54, 78
Wedmore, Peace of: 52, 54
weights and measures: 56
Wessex: *see* Saxon Kingdoms
Whitby, Synod of: 40, *41*
William the Conqueror (William I): 3, 48, *60*, 67*f*, 70*ff*, 74, *75*, 76, *77f*, 80*f*, 84*f*
William Rufus: 72
Witan, the: 57, 61, 66*ff*, 70, 80
Woden: 35, 41

Europe

NORWAY

SWEDEN

IRELAND

NORTH SEA

UNITED KINGDOM

NETHERLANDS

GERMANY

FRANCE

Rome